Three Mothers
(and a camel)

Three Mothers (and a camel)

Notes to my Mother-in-Law

and

How Many Camels
Are There in Holland?

Phyllida Law

Mrs Thompson

The Jesuits say, 'Give me a boy for his first seven years and I'll give you the man.' What if you gave them a girl? Discuss.

My mother Meg was given me till the age of seven, at which point war broke out. The second one. I can remember where she sat to tell me I was to be an 'evacuee'. I was to leave home and stay in the country away from something called 'Air Raid'. 'Life is made up of moments', and that was one of them.

My evacuee school was a dozen pupils in a dining room. It was made clear that I did not belong. I was a wee Glasgow 'keelie' who caught fleas, lost her gas mask and thought Adam and Eve lived in Kirkintilloch. I responded by becoming shy, secretive and anxious to please – and a telltale too.

I was moved to another school as the only boarder. Looking back I feel bereft, seeing an isolated little person. But I loved it. I loved the school room. It was entirely mine of an evening, a large room lined with bookshelves amongst which I found an ancient medical dictionary. Reading avidly I discovered that, amongst other things, I was suffering from a sexually transmitted disease. My friend Isobel Hebblethwaite said I had caught it from a loo seat and would probably die young. I thought I'd better not tell my mother, who in any case wasn't there, and I wouldn't tell Miss Jenny, my teacher, as I didn't think sex was one of her subjects. I decided simply to devote my life to the healing of the human race. A Scottish Mother Teresa. With a stethoscope.

After my book-lined classroom I was sent to a fully-furnished boarding school with 40-minute lessons, dinner bells, hockey, lacrosse and 'don't run in the corridors'. Mother became a treat. She was like Christmas, turning up at half term bringing gifts: treacle toffee, sox and my first bra (a Kestos, all buttons and elastic, which she waved at me amongst a cloud of classmates). Such embarrassments aside, the agony of her going was difficult to endure with dignity.

I'm not sure boarding school was brilliant preparation for motherhood. I have even envied baby chimpanzees hooked so conveniently on their mother's hip. We all learn from example, don't we? What's more, they get a comprehensive sex education. My mother, daughter of the Manse, had none. Grannie first advised her daughters that on marrying they should buy nighties that buttoned down the front. I fared better with my medical dictionary, snogging at the back of a touring bus, and the Jean Anouilh play about Orpheus and Eurydice (*Point of Departure*).

Flying in the face of reason, we got married on the morning of a matinée day when we were both in *A Midsummer Night's Dream*. We thought we'd better practise birth control for a bit, so we bought an odd little swivelling metallic calendar from an advert in *The Spectator*. It didn't work. So we had Emma.

I told my mother I couldn't bring up this tiny creature as I had no opinions or convictions of any sort. She said I had. She said I'd soon find out. I was a weather vane in a gale-force wind. What was a mother? What was a father? We made it up as we went along, cherry-picking from our past.

Emma was an elegant, independent baby with a gift for getting out of her cot. Sophie the Second didn't bother. She studied us from a distance with her enormous black eyes and now and again let out a deep, drunken giggle. We used to bribe Em to make her laugh. She took her duties as the eldest very seriously. I still feel guilty about saying to her, unthinkingly, 'We are going to have another baby.' Another? Instead of me? The English language is a minefield. So is parenthood, isn't it?

I soothed Em as a baby with Rose Hip Syrup, endlessly advertised for babies, and vitamin C. It's the syrup that's the culprit. It produced brown dots of decay on Em's front teeth and the dentist said he would give her implants when she was seventeen. I remember shaking helplessly for days, cleaning, wiping and weeping. It was fine. And no one advertises Rose Hip Syrup any more.

Sophie got eczema and a vicious diet. We would take fruit and small brown sandwiches for any celebration instead of sweeties. Other children were impressed.

Bringing up children was in some way easier when the world was younger and you could leave your baby in its pram outside the butcher's. *Outside.* You could keep an eye on it through the window whilst it ate lumps of the bread you had just bought next door, and offered it to passersby.

There was nothing electronic anywhere, although I think the butcher had a calculator. My husband was apprenticed to the village butcher when he was a little lad. Indeed he was brought up by his village, and it became a very vivid strand in our lives. Tea with Grannie Annie meant washing your hands, sitting up straight at the table, being handed bread and butter first, and speaking only when spoken to. Then, after cake, you said, 'Please may I be excused?' and went wild in her cottage garden. My mother Meg was another country. She was a loch and hills, fishing, splashing and 'Spag Bol'.

*

That's the easy bit over, isn't it? Then you come to school. I don't ever want to go through that again, though I distantly do with my grand-children. It would have been easier for me to understand my daughters' lives if they could have followed in my footsteps.

There were two objections. How could you send your children away? Evacuate them aged seven? My poor mother. And then there was the money. We had none. That put the tin lid on it and made our path simpler, I suppose. They went to the wonder-fully walkable local, which looked like a detention centre for the criminally insane. It was brilliant.

And there were boys. Bliss. It wasn't long before we came up against what Alan Bennett calls, in his play *Forty Years On*, 'the problem of your body'. A schoolmaster instructing his pupils on 'down there' says, 'It isn't pretty but it's there for a purpose.'

I think I drew pictures. My husband was blunt and I did the diagrams. I think we laughed. I hope we laughed. I mean, sex is ridiculous behaviour from adults who tell you not to pick your nose. And it has to be repeated endlessly, doesn't it?

Emma, aged eight, once asked Alec Guinness about the details and he gave her a calm and accurate response. Very helpful, though I felt a bit faint. Sophie, then aged five, listened gravely, fixing him with her headlamp eyes. Unblinking. We never knew she had whites to them until we took her up in an aeroplane.

My grandson Walter, whilst at school, did a picture of a lighthouse which his teacher took to be quite another thing. She was not amused. Such a pity. A good laugh with a teacher on this difficult subject would be very valuable. I think she missed a trick.

Love – that over-used four-letter word – was another stumbler. My ma always said your heart had to be broken ten times before it was any use to you as a heart. I think that's a bit severe. Five times?

Sophie was once ditched by her beloved in a letter sent to her on holiday. Her grief was terrible to behold. He wrote that it was impossible to continue with their relationship as she was far too young. She was eleven. He was fourteen. I thought she would never recover.

But I can't forgive him for leaving before his grandchildren arrived. I find that particularly painful. Like four knives in the heart. He was such great casting for a granddad. He would have taught them all fishing and how to skin a rabbit. They would learn how to make bacon and tomato 'sclunge' and fry cheese on a tin plate. They'd learn long words like obdurate and antimacassar. *Monty Python* would be required viewing and they'd know where he hid the chocolate.

He had an original mind and he looked for it in other people, especially his daughters. I envied them, as I improvised my form of motherhood. I seemed to have very little to go on. I only hope it was enough. I'll ask...

Sophie

The lady said, 'Write something about your mum. A couple of "funny anecdotes"...' Oh dear, I thought, where do I begin? A mum is a whole world if you're lucky, not just a single landmass. How many words? How rude can they be?

It was becoming a mum that made me begin to see that Mum hadn't been born a mum. She was just like me – a woman who had brought two curious creatures into this world, literally squeezed them out shrieking and groaning after having sexual relations with that fellow who was my dad... Let's not go there.

There she is. There we all are, us mums, making it up as we go along, responding as wisely as we can to these individuals who have struggled out of our bodies just slightly less alarmingly than the alien in that film.

So what is she like, my spaceship woman, who landed me here like a wet fish on the shore? Well. My mum was a very steady girl. Golly. Well done, Mum. How did you do that? She was never shouty. Except twice, I remember, and crikey was I scared.

Mum set the scene with visuals and smells. She'd wrap our presents in brown paper and paint beautiful pictures on them. She'd always make sure there was a cooking smell when we came in from school. She'd leave on all the lights on purpose. Our godfather Ron would say the house looked like a boat in a dark sea when you walked up the road at night.

She was a working mum and she was a wonderful mess. I liked to be in her dressing room at nights with the play feeding in on the tannoy, hearing her out there. I'd clear her chaotic make-up space, line up her lipsticks and blow the sweet face powder about. So she was very there and then sometimes she wasn't. But you knew she was somewhere doing her thing. And she'd leave little presents if she was away on tour or something. My favourite was a tiny jar of Pond's Cold Cream. It was like having a little piece of her.

Mum wasn't very physical and then out of the blue she would grab you and squidge you sooo hard, chanting 'Passion! Passion!' through gritted teeth like a lunatic. You could feel her tight with love.

I don't remember ever really clashing with Mum. She didn't like confrontation, I learnt later. I think I sensed her tiller in the water doing its mum thing, shifting kindly in all the currents that make a family. Keeping things steady for Dad, we found out later too.

Sometimes I struggled to explain myself to Mum and worried I was an utter loon. And sometimes I think I scared her when I wanted to show her my feelings. It felt like an oblique challenge to her own very hidden depths.

She was an evacuee. Now I see all those feelings packed tightly in her gas-mask bag, or deep in the pockets that went with her to strange 'aunties' and then boarding school. I wish I could have been that little girl's friend.

Mum's a great laugher. That's her way through. She flings her head back and just laughs.

Mum walked me down the aisle when I got married, her head so high and laughing.

Mum loves to lower the tone and will always find her way through the really sore bits by finding the absurd.

Mum pretends she doesn't like lots of things – like Shakespeare, just because it's anarchic to say that in our profession. (I know she likes him a little bit.)

Mum says she's a snob, and she is!

Mum looked after my dad's mum and then her mum, which makes her an almighty mum in my book.

Mum pretends she doesn't have opinions but I know she does, very strong ones. She says when she is Queen she will ban Starbucks and leisure clothing.

Mum is from a generation that was engendered with extraordinary stoicism. She never complains, not even in the height of grief.

She is so brave. She just gets on with it. She is so brave.

Mum is a great beauty.

Mum is great fun to drink with. Eat with. Be with. Drink with.

My boys adore my mum; she is their 'Fifi'.

Mum looks most herself in Scotland amongst the hills of her home. She looks like a piece of the hillside that's fallen off in a high wind and loves wearing the same clothes until they stand up on their own.

Mum says she is a martyr to her wind.

Mum can't ever say she is proud of my sister and me because she feels that's a bit big-headed on her behalf.

Well, I can say I'm proud of *her* cos she's my *mum*.

Oh, I am proud of her.

Rattlingly proud.

Emma

It's rather difficult to write about one's mother while she's still alive. There could be consequences. But the first thing that pops into my head is that she's a tough act to follow. Long ago I remember deciding that I could never be as good, kind, wise, loving and generally brilliant and gorgeous as her. It's taken me over half a century to stop trying.

Stepping back, I see her more clearly. I remember her giving me a birthday tea when I was about five or six – she baked scones and fairy cakes, dressed up as a waitress and served us as if we were in a Lyon's Corner House. I think her hat was made from a doily.

When we were ill or hurt she always soothed us in Gaelic. She sang us lullabies and rubbed hot oil on our chests in winter.

The only time she has ever evinced pride in something I've done was when I told her, backstage at a Footlights gig, that I had received a good result in my degree. She screeched for joy and I felt ten miles high. She expresses pride in her grand-children, though, which prompted my sister to suggest, with benevolent tartness, that perhaps it (pride) skipped a generation.

We've worked together many times, and I once wrote a very long monologue for a TV programme back in the day when autocue didn't exist. I'd learnt it but it was full of repetition and proved rather difficult. Mum, who was in the show as well, watched every take and when I got it wrong for the umpteenth time, she marched over the stage with her skirts pulled up over her bum to cheer me up. She'd forgotten that she wasn't wearing knickers under her tights though. It got me through, I can tell you. And the crew.

She's a stoic but her stoicism is rooted in humour. I have never witnessed her grieving in a life dotted with rich opportunities for grief. But I have seen her laughing a lot.

I have profound respect for her brain and as we have, one way or the other, been very much together since my father died, I credit her with the development of my own writing. I used to do a bit of stand-up and I would rehearse every set in front of her, cold, in the kitchen, and she was startlingly accurate about what worked and what didn't.

It's difficult for people who know her now to imagine but, like her mother before her, she could be fierce. Once, when I was seven or so, I picked a bluebell from a garden as we were walking down the road. Mum marched me, sobbing with fear (me, not her), to the door of the house and made me confess and give it back. Guilt's big in our family.

Dad once said to me, 'You're a taker, Em, and I'm a taker, but your mother is a giver.' That wasn't much of a help, I have to tell you. When we moved from our flat into a house which was only round the corner she did a lot of the removals herself. I can see her walking up the hill wearing a lot of khaki and a saucepan on her head. When we were little she was always stripping something made of old pine.

I did witness her, on occasion, sacrificing her own pleasure for the sake of my grandmothers or her ailing brother or her sick husband or her two demanding daughters and, as she says, it could be construed as a fine way to avoid living your own life.

But it doesn't quite wash. She has always worked, with hiatuses of course, but she has always gone back to work – as an actor and now as an author. I do concede, however, that it may have helped her to avoid another relationship. Some years ago she went on a date with a friend's father. I think he tried to kiss her in the cab. She's never recovered.

Maybe the qualities in her writing describe her better than I can: it's spare, full of curious and telling detail and mysterious ellipses, very funny, touching without trying to be, connected to every little action of every little day, and in character quite unlike anything else I have ever read. Except perhaps Montaigne, who was equally intrigued by the quotidian business of being human.

The best bit of the day is around about 6pm when one of us rings her, says, 'The bar's open,' and hangs up. By the time I've poured a slug of decent red wine, she's putting her key in the door. I'll hand over the glass and she will invariably say, 'Ooh. I've been looking forward to that all day.' Then we share the news.

Notes to my
mother-in-law

For my daughters

PROLOGUE

Annie, my mother-in-law, lived with us for seventeen years and was picture-book perfect.

She washed on Monday, ironed on Tuesday. Wednesday was bedrooms, Thursday baking, Friday fish and floors, Saturday polishing, particularly the brass if it was 'looking red' at her. Sunday was God and sewing. She had a framed print of *The Light of the World* on her bedroom wall and her drawers were full of crochet hooks and knitting needles. She could turn the heel of a sock and the collar of a shirt. She made rock cakes, bread pudding and breast of lamb with barley, and she would open a tin of condensed milk and hide it at the back of the fridge with a spoon in it if things were going badly in our world. She came to us when things had stopped going well in hers.

The rented cottage she left had the rose 'New Dawn' curling over and around a front door she never used. All of life flowed towards the back door and led into the kitchen and her cupboards full of jams and bottled fruit. Her little parlour was all table and dresser, with a fireplace full of wild flowers in a cracked china soup tureen. She wallpapered the front room every spring. Three walls with one pattern and the fourth to contrast. But what she loved most was her wood pile and her long, narrow garden where the hedges were full of old toys and rusty tricycles. Here, my children used to hide on fine summer nights, sitting straight-backed in their flannel pyjamas between rows of beans to eat furry red and gold gooseberries, rasps that weren't ripe and rhubarb dipped into an egg cup of sugar.

All she managed to bring with her to London were two white china oven dishes, half a dozen pocket editions of Shakespeare, her button box, her silver thimble, a wooden darning mushroom, a large bundle of knitting needles tied with tape and a tiny pewter pepper pot, which became a vital prop at our midday planning meetings.

LUNCH.

I have never been able to take lunch seriously, but for Gran it was crucial. She never took anything more than two Rich Tea biscuits and one mug of tea for breakfast, so around noon, depending on her chores, she would say her stomach thought her throat had been cut and come downstairs. When I heard the tap of her wide wedding ring on the banister rail I would strain the potatoes.

The menu was a challenge. I'd learnt from her son that lettuce was 'rabbit food'. (Gran could skin a rabbit as if she was removing its cardigan.) Favourites were fried cheese, Yorkshire pudding, onion gravy, dumplings, stuffed heart and kidneys cooked pink – don't make the plates too hot.

I was nervous. I had discovered garlic. I called baby marrows 'courgettes' and pea pods 'mangetout'. I ate salad with French dressing, spread marmalade on toasted cheese, and there was no Bisto in the house. I often feel that food can be as big a stumbler as politics and thought Gran and I might be incompatible in the kitchen – but when lunch was up to scratch her appreciation was so utterly delightful that the meal became a game I loved to win. I planned sudden treats of stale cake – kept cake was more digestible – winkles eaten with a pin or fresh-boiled crab.

Curious about the pretty little pewter pepper pot, I discovered it had come from the Blue Coat School where her father had been a cobbler. Gran had been one of four children, and life couldn't have been easy for she learnt when she was very young how to pawn the candlesticks and bring her mother jugs of beer from the pub.

Her country life began when there was an epidemic of scarlet fever and the Blue Coat School moved out of London. There wasn't enough work so her father was made redundant and Gran went into service at the age of fourteen. She had a scar on one hand from when an irate employer had biffed her with the handle of a broom she had left standing on its bristles. I loved her stories of cruel cooks and horrid housekeepers. It was like having lunch with Catherine Cookson.

Between the juicy bits we organized our days, and it was some while before I realized she was just a bit, as she would say, 'Mutt and Jeff'. It was quite a few years before we all grasped that shouting wasn't enough. After some hilarious misunderstandings, and to avoid confusion, I stuck comprehensive lists on the fridge door beside a large calendar marked with coloured crayons. It still wasn't enough. Gran always said she'd rather be blind than deaf, and aware at last that she was becoming increasingly isolated, I began to write out the day's gossip at the kitchen table, putting my notes by her bed before I went to mine.

One night my husband wandered off to his, muttering darkly that I spent so much time each evening writing to Gran that I could have written a book – 'And illustrated it!' he shouted from the stairs.

Here it is.

Your suspenders were 50p. John Barnes only had pink ones. Got these up Post Office. Change on kitchen table.

———·—·———

The chiropodist is calling at 1.30 p.m. tomorrow (Tuesday). Inconvenient creature. We will have to lunch early and you can have a snooze when he's gone.

———·—·———

Dad is golfing tomorrow. Emma is going to spend the day at the library. I think Sophie and I should be home about teatime. Lamb stew on stove. Kettle on about quarter to five? Ta.

———·—·———

Dear, I honestly don't think they would make a mistake like that. They only took a wax impression of the deaf ear, and that must be the one you are meant to put it in I think. Why not try Vaseline? I don't think licking it is a good idea.

———

I'll get some pearl-barley tomorrow, Gran. Sorry about that, the kids hate it, you see. It's a bit slimy. I suppose it *is* very good for you. There was a woman in Ardentinny who used to boil it and strain it and drink the water from it every day. I think she had something wrong with her kidneys.

———

The piano tuner is coming tomorrow at 3 p.m. so when you are dusting don't bother to put back the photos as such. He usually moves everything himself but I'm not sure if he can see terribly well. He seems never to look me straight in the eye and there is something odd about his glasses. It would be awful if he dropped Churchill. Let's give him the last of the rock-cakes. I'll be home so there is no need to stay downstairs for the bell.

———•———

Dusters aren't all that expensive. Perhaps we could use that stockingette stuff the butcher sells? Don't sacrifice your bloomers in this rash manner. Heaven knows where we'll get interlocking cotton now Pontings is closed. I might try that haberdasher's next to Woolworths in Hampstead. She still keeps those skeins of plaited darning wool. Last time I was in she told me she was one of the first sales ladies in John Lewis. Apparently they lived over the shop in those days in some sort of hostel, which was very strictly run. She got something like 17/6 per week, I think. You probably got that for a year.

———•———

Listen, we must practise. That Mr Parnes said we must. Ten minutes every day in a carpeted room, he said. Preferably with curtains. So I will come upstairs with your tea tomorrow and we will have ten minutes' practice in your room. The kitchen is far too noisy.

I have to sit *directly* opposite you and speak slowly. As soon as you get used to my voice I'll send someone else up with tea and we'll do a few minutes longer each day. It is essential that we go about this sensibly.

You may have to hold it in your ear for the moment and I'll ring Mr Parnes about other fitting arrangements. He agrees that the main disadvantage is the tiny switch. The tips of one's fingers do go dead after a certain age and how one is supposed to adjust the beastly thing when there is no feeling in one's fingers I can't think.

I'll mark the little wheel thing with a biro when you feel it's about right and we can adjust it before you put it in. That's settled. Practice will commence at 5 p.m. precisely tomorrow, Wednesday 9th inst., 1978.

Thank you very much, Gran. I will go round to Kingston's tomorrow as they close Thursday afternoon. Is it collar you want? Or is it slipper? Green or smoked? Middle gammon is something like 84p per lb. It'll be a great help to have something to cut cold on Saturday.

I found your splint in the hall drawer.

———•·———

I tell you what I suggest. Just give up knitting for a while and see if that doesn't help. The physiotherapist I went to for my shoulders thought knitting was really bad for you. Especially with aluminium needles. Aluminium gets a very bad press these days. Mother has changed to enamel because she thinks Uncle Arthur is going potty. She says if you put cold water in a hot aluminium pan it pits the metal and you are swallowing chemicals with every mouthful. She says Aunt Avril used to put bicarbonate in with rhubarb and cabbage and an evil green slime used to rise to the top, which was poisonous. And that's what's the matter with Uncle Arthur. I could suggest a few other things.

Uncle Arthur

I didn't know Aunt Min was deaf. I thought she just had diabetes. You must ask her how she gets on with the NHS box model. Maybe the knobs are bigger. Let me put a new battery in for you. They are such wretched fiddly little things and apparently it's only too easy to leave them switched on when not in use. Mr Parnes says one should last you six weeks, but you could have left it on overnight, and that would explain the difficulty. I had a deaf landlady when I was a student and she was forever leaving her apparatus on, when it would give piercing shrieks and she couldn't hear and we would all have to look for the box. It was nearly as big as a wireless.

If there was a thunderstorm she used to unplug herself, cover all the mirrors with dishcloths and shut herself in the larder under the stairs. Nice woman.

Now, don't forget to make a list of worries for Mr Parnes and we will sort them all out on Friday morning. I'm afraid your routine will be very much disturbed. Let's do the floors on Saturday and the brass before we go on Friday. Variety is the slice of life, as Aunt Avril used to say.

We used the wooden knitting needles for propping up the house-plants. Remember?

Nothing much of note to report. This weather will kill us all. Take an extra pill. Be a devil. Called on Mrs Wilson as I passed to check on her wrist. She broke it on Tuesday, did I tell you? She tripped on one of those proud paving stones opposite number 48, and in order to stop herself from falling she put out her hand to steady herself against one of the lime trees.

'It just snapped like a twig,' she said.

Being Mrs Wilson, she clattered on up the road and did the shopping before stumbling back home with a wrist like a whoopee cushion. The doctor showed her the X-ray. She says it looked like a crushed digestive biscuit.

'I'm sorry to have to tell you, Mrs Wilson,' he said, 'that you will never have a normal wrist again.'

'My dear,' said Mrs Wilson, clutching my arm, 'I'm deformed.'

Boot has been sick under the hall table.

———•———

All set for tomorrow, then? We should leave by 10.30 a.m. so we'll have to forget the brass this week. It seems very early to leave for a twelve o'clock appointment but I'm worried about the parking. Gloucester Place is one way and tremendously long as streets go, which means we'll have to go right down Baker Street to turn into it and cruise along trying to find the right number. Let's hope it's not raining but the forecast is frightful. I think the brolly is in the car.

I'll try to park as close to the house as possible, of course, but what we will have to do is to stop the car by the door and see you inside. Then, while you sit in the waiting room for a bit, I'll park the car comfortably and come back to go in with you. We should have hankies in handbags and some wine gums. Also a biro for the Daily Mail crossword in case we are kept waiting. Most importantly, do not forget the box with deaf-aid, batteries old and new, and the grotty earpiece. Any change you have in your purse will likely come in handy. I think we'll need two-bob bits for the meter. Lots of them.

I plan to make a slight detour on the way home to pick up fish and chips.

Friday!

Apparently if I fill in the bit on the back with all the extenuating circumstances I may not have to pay so hang on to your pension for now, darling.

The wee warden was very stricken. He would never have given us one if we'd got there in time but he was writing it out when I arrived, and once they've started they can't stop. They have to complete the beastly thing, you see, because it's numbered and in triplicate or whatever and he can't destroy it, or the Authorities would run him over or something. He's written our story on the back of this piece and I'm to do the same with mine and they will review the situation. He says we might get away with it and we are to apply for one of those orange disabled badges. This means a visit to the doctor and the town hall where apparently they look at you in case you're a fraud. We'll do it. Then we'll park on yellow lines and block bus lanes.

———

Our Mr Parnes is ex-RAF, did you know?

Could you hear him or were you just pretending? You said, 'Yes,' a lot.

I suspect him of speaking quietly to test your apparatus.

He says you mustn't wash it, darling. No harm done apparently but the battery had to be replaced again. Do you remember when I washed the coffee-grinder and wrecked the engine?

We'll start the Waxol treatment tonight. He says we should use it for a week each month and I will check the earpiece with cotton-wool and a toothpick.

Mr P put a biro mark on the earpiece and it's miles further up the wheel so it's nearly at full blast and I am going to fix it with some sticky tape as I think it is liable to slip. There is just a possibility that we may have to pad one leg of your specs.

Maybe it was a bit silly of us to leave it on in the car. It was Mr P's idea but then he probably doesn't drive a Volkswagen. The plan is to train your ears again to accept different levels of sound. We'll start in the garden with the birds and *progress* to washing-machines and Hoovers.

I notice that when he plays selected noises on his machine you seem to nod more often at the treble end of the scale, which accounts for the fact that you can still hear me calling you for lunch.

Also, I thought he was reassuring and sensible on the subject of nerves. Apparently that's why you hear the first words of a sentence and then everything fades. You have always said it was fright that stops you hearing Fred on the phone. 'Hello' is fine and then it's pure panic. It's the ability to *relax* and *concentrate* at the same time, which is needed here. Good training for tight-rope walking. I always do deep-breathing when I'm nervous. It was a terrific help in my driving test but God knows what it would do to a telephone conversation.

———

Everything is easier in a familiar place with a familiar face. Then you can sit and relax and we must sit directly in front of you and in a good light. If you can't see someone it's very difficult to hear them.

Mrs Wilson says that's why the minister is difficult to hear, and he will put his hand over his

chins with the padded toe and saying, 'QX, QX, QX.' Wonderful woman.

So, anyway, I've buried it all. I expect the minister's cats will dig it all up. No sooner do I turn fresh earth up than they all waltz in and pee. He has four, you know, and I saw the big ginger one with feathers sticking out of its mouth. There's a fiendish wall-eyed tom from the flats who dug up all my hyacinths and the banana skins under our roses.

the ministers cat

Mother's neighbour at Ardentinny went all round the coast to pick up a dead rat found on the beach so that she could bury it under her rosebed. They'll eat anything, she says. Roses, that is.

I tipped your button box on to the Times to search for curtain hooks. Found plastic *and* brass.

You know, it's an historic collection. There's that big green button which belonged to the first coat we bought you at C & A's. You were horrified by the price but it was a great success. Where the hell is it? Did we leave it in Scotland?

Soph came in and started a personal treasure hunt. She has chosen eight different coloured buttons and is presently cutting off the ones on her pink cardigan to replace them with this rainbow set.

Good grief.

Don't, whatever you do, put your hands into the water in the sink in the washroom. I've got pieces off the stove soaking in a strong solution of Flash. It would play hell with your psoriasis.

I will do the fridge and oven in the morning and clean under the bath. Must get bulk buy of bicarb. I gave Eleanor our last packet for her cystitis so I'll use the box for your teeth and replace it, if you don't mind?

I couldn't get Garibaldi biscuits up at Flax's and I couldn't get Min cream. Mrs Venning says it seems to have disappeared off the shelves.

Met Mr Wilson up the hill today and stopped to ask after Mrs Wilson's wrist. She is doing very well but of course he has to do the shopping for her and it hurts his poor feet. Anyway, we were happily passing the time of day when I noticed he had a little flower petal stuck to his cheek. So, without thinking, I put my hand up and picked it off. My dear, it was only a piece of pink toilet paper he'd stuck on a shaving cut. I was mortified.

Talking of toilet paper, I got much the cheapest buy at the International. Quite pleased with myself, and then I had to pay a fine on the library books. They won't let you off if you are an OAP. They say they might if there were 'special circumstances'. They say they are human.

Which reminds me, I've had to pay that parking fine after all. Don't you think that's MEAN?

Got Garibaldis at the International.

I know what it is, Gran. It's Boot. She *will* eat spiders. Every so often she has an overdose and throws up on your bedcovers. It's all arms and legs. I think she eats daddy-long-legs as well. It'll be easy to wash out and we can freshen it up outside on the first fine day.

I hoovered under our bed this morning by the way. Found the following: one sock, seven pence, a dod of makeup-covered cotton-wool, two golf tees, one biro and a cardboard box of curtain rings.

———————

Well, I don't understand it. She seems all right generally, doesn't she?

When she howls like that I can't bear it. I've put a bundle of old Daily Mails in the broom cupboard so if she starts yelling try to get one under her.

She's taken all the polish off the parquet in the hall and there is an ugly stain on the tiles under the kitchen table, which I just can't shift. I dread her throwing up on the carpet. We will never get the smell out. Every time the car gets hot there it is again. The unmistakable Boot pong.

Actually I apologised to Mrs Wilson when I gave her a lift the other day and the smell turned out to be some Charentais melon she had in her shopping bag.

———

Drops for the last time tomorrow morning. We mustn't forget to ask the doctor about the form for a disabled badge. He has to sign it.

Appointment 5.20 p.m. We'll leave on the hour.

Actually, before we leave let's write down anything you want to ask the doctor. We mustn't waste our visit. All my symptoms fly out of the window as soon as I'm in the door.

Have you enough ointment?

Have you enough pills?

Are you still worried about your eyes?

Do you need any sweeties?

We can pass the sweet shop as we come home. Mrs Estherson says we won't get coconut logs any more because the Scottish firm of Ferguson's in Glasgow has closed down. She says she thinks she can get us Richmond Assorted.

Mother sends love. She says the ferry was off last week because a jellyfish got stuck in the works.

———•———

Well done, darling. Thank Heaven that's over, and I expect you'll feel the benefit tomorrow. He says there is no infection whatsoever and just a tiny bit of inflammation from the wax. Keep a wee bit of warm cotton-wool in it overnight. He says it won't affect your aid, and you can go on using it safely. Apparently the wax has absolutely nothing to do with it.

Also, it's natural for syringing to make you feel dizzy and a bit seedy. And it's natural to be scared. He wondered if you ought to have a blood test you looked so pale but I knew it was terror. Also I don't think the water was warm and he was so enthusiastic that he squirted it all over his suit. Serves him right, I say. Never mind, it needed doing. I held the kidney bowl under your ear and it was spectacular. Reminded me we ought to get the chimney swept this year.

While you were recovering there I asked him about deaf-aids and he agreed immediately to an appointment for you at the Royal Free. He says the box models are much easier for elderly people to manage because the controls are larger. It's just circulation, I think. He thought we could stitch a pocket to your pinny on the bodice somewhere so the box wasn't under the table when you sat down, but I think that would muffle the microphone. He said he would certainly sign a form for our disabled badge. He doesn't keep them. You can pick them up at the town hall, he says.

We are getting one! When we get one I can *drive* you to the doctor's and we can park in the Finchley Road, which means we won't have to gallop across the road like that. Those traffic lights don't give us half enough time to cross, do they? I remember I used to find that with the pram.

Oh, and by the way, he has had a very good wheeze about your pills. You can get the same medicine in *liquid* form, and he says he has an idea it works quicker. It must take ages for those depth-charges to dissolve in your stomach. No more choking them down or struggling to halve them.

The doctor said those large pills should be easier to swallow but Mother says Uncle Arthur keeps a hammer in his bedroom to smash his into little bits. He has trouble with his oesophagus, though. Not sure I've spelt that correctly.

Uncle Arthur advancing on a large pill

The vet says it's fur ball. Why should she suddenly get fur ball? I didn't know ordinary black bring-you-luck type cats ever got fur ball. I thought it was only those fluffy Persian people. In fact, Dad and I paid £3 for a tiny bad-tempered Persian kitten from that pet shop in Parkway when something about the lecture we had on fur ball made us go back for a refund and buy Ms Boot, who was only thirty bob.

Oh, well. Change of life, I suppose. Apparently we have to brush her regularly. She is to be given a dose of liquid paraffin every day for a week, and then once a week as a general rule. Good grief. She seems quite to enjoy the brushing if it's not too near her old scar but I don't know how to get her to take the paraffin. I put one lot in her milk and she stepped in it.

I rang the vet and he says to squeeze her jaws at the corner when she will be forced to grin and then someone can fling it down on a teaspoon. Not much success so far. We've put the liquid paraffin in the cupboard above the fireplace by the way in case we get into a muddle – tho', mind you, Mother used to use it for cooking during the war. She made a wonderful orange sponge with it when we were short of fat. Everyone loved it and it was beautifully light and airy so her cousin Joan ordered one for her baby's christening, and all the baby guests loved it too, with very unfortunate results.

Funny to think of those days. It was 2 oz butter per person per week, wasn't it? When we were staying at Granny's Flora, the maid, would put our butter ration on little dishes by our places so as to be strictly fair, but Granny used to steal bits and give it to Major Reddick, an officer who was billeted on her, and whom she adored. Us kids loathed him. He used to take his teeth out before a meal, wrap them in his khaki hanky and keep them in his pocket till he was finished, when he would replace the teeth and dry his hanky before the fire.

Frightful creature. Flora said he wore a corset. Every morning after breakfast he would rise from the table and say, without fail, 'Let's see what the King has got for us to do today.' Mother says he attacked her in the morning room and she told him she would scream for Mama.

'What's the matter with you?' he said. 'Don't you like men?'

I think uniforms are bad for people.

———•———

Darling, we are all terribly sorry. Truly.

I absolutely promise we were not laughing at you, and it was all my fault. Well, it was my fault originally but then Dad started making cheeky remarks and we all got hysterical.

What happened was this: everyone was discussing the merits of bran for constipation. Dad said he knew you hadn't been, but I wasn't constipated, was I, so why did I take it?

So I said, 'Piles.' Well, you know I get piles sometimes, don't you? They started with Emma. Haven't had them for ages but I take bran every day in case. It's quite fashionable.

So then I told them a dreadful story I have never told anyone before.

Last summer, when you and I were visiting Mother, I was suddenly painfully afflicted, and there was no bran in the house. Uncle Arthur won't tolerate it. Mother has tried to give him All Bran for breakfast but he just sits there with bits sticking out of his mouth like a bad-tempered bird building a nest. So, anyway, I had read somewhere that a very good remedy was to put a clove of garlic up your bum. So I did. For about a week – well, every night for about a week. The trick is to get rid of it in the morning, but on the day we drove back south I didn't have time to go to the loo properly and the garlic was still up there, if you see what I mean.

Uncle Arthur & ALL-BRAN

Well, we left very early to catch the first ferry and round about the Lake District with no windows open I'm afraid I was forced to fart and the smell was simply frightful. You were very alarmed and thought there was something wrong with the car. I told you we were passing through farmland and it was probably chemical fertiliser.

Of course, when I was telling this disgusting tale, everyone looked at you and fell about. Do you see? I know you thought we were laughing at *you*, but really we were laughing at *me* and I somehow couldn't get you to hear and Dad was being very wicked and making matters worse.

Please forgive me. I hope you believe we would never talk about you to your face and laugh like that. It's just so impossible when there are a lot of people at table to persuade everyone to talk one at a time and of course your box picks up all the cutlery noise.

It must be horrible for you. I am so sorry. We'd all hate it if you didn't come down to meals, darling. Please don't do that.

Mrs Wilson is fine now, but a bit stiff. Mr Wilson drove to Glastonbury last week and brought her back some Holy Water in a petrol can.

She is keen to stick her wrist in that shrine somewhere near Sidmouth. There's a sort of hole in a bit of stone and you put the injured limb through it and pray to some saint. Saint Monica or somebody, it could be. Anyway, it's a woman.

———•———

Gran, have you seen a set of keys anywhere?

———•———

Not *this* Tuesday, darling. Next Tuesday. Sorry, sorry, sorry. It was Sunday when I said it and I meant not this Tuesday coming but next Tuesday, i.e. the Tuesday in the week following next Sunday. Oh, curses, it's one of those misunderstandings like the pronunciation of 'scone', and whether a crumpet is a big flat dark thing with holes in it or a wee fat white thing with holes in it, or whether treacle is syrup or the other way round or neither. How long were you sitting with your feet in a bowl?

————

Mother is in a frantic state. You know the stray cat I told you about? Well, not only did it give Uncle Arthur asthma but it started to get some sort of discharge from its ears so she took it to the vet and he advised her to have it put down. He said it would be kinder to do it at once so she left it with him and came home. Now, of course, Ada tells her that the doctor has lost his tabby and is searching the coast. My dear, she may have murdered the doctor's cat.

————

Nothing to report.

Dad used some of your psoriasis cream on that rough patch on his shin and it's gone. Brilliant.

The minister's wife came home from a late Thursday bulk shopping trip and dropped a bottle of whisky and six eggs while unloading.

the whisky cost £6.98

No, nobody was hurt. It's just that whisky costs £6.98.

Hi, Gran! The doorbell will ring between 2 and 2.30 p.m. Don't be alarmed, it's only Mr Venning come to change the lock. If you have your nap in the chair in the kitchen after lunch you will hear the bell and no bother. I've told Syd he must wait awhile for you to answer so don't rush to the door whatever you do. Absolutely no need.

I've told Gerry just to leave my order on the window-sill, well wrapped against Boot, but she never uses the letter-box now. Not since that day she got stuck. (I remember one holiday in Skye Mother put a Queen of Puddings on the window ledge and a sheep ate the lot!)

Talking of which, lunch is on the stove. Plus lots of rice pudding with a dod of jam (yours).

I shall be home by 4.30 at the very latest, which gives us ample time to get to the doctor at 5 p.m. Your raincoat is on the hallstand. Looks like we'll need it. The kids will have tea mashed by the time we get back.

———

So it was Mr Venning who finished the rock-cakes! You'll have to make more as I'm hoping against hope that the window-cleaner will come next week.

Nice that Syd had some tea. That was a very good move. Mrs Venning told me about the rock-cakes when I was in to get Brillo Clearaway for the bath. She says Syd has a very sweet tooth. He gave her 50p to go to Alexis for a piece of cheesecake and two Bath buns for his lunch. Well, my dear, she only got a *small* piece of cheesecake for the money. 'Where are the buns?' cried Syd.

'He lives in the past,' says Mrs V.

She tells me old Mr Samuel's grocery is opening shortly as a centre for water beds. I ask you. I expect kids will go in and wreck the place with a packet of pins. Mrs V is highly amused.

Syd says the crack above your door is because all the houses are slipping downhill. And, of course, so is the roof, and the plumbing is original. 'Never mind,' said Mrs Venning. 'You're sitting on a fortune, Mrs T.'

———•—•———

Escott's are coming to turn the stair carpet on Wednesday week. That's a week this coming

Wednesday. Dad has nailed down that waggly stair-rod for safety and they will do it properly when they come. Mr E says we could never do it ourselves and there are three steps which are dangerously thread-bare so take care just now.

You will be pleased to hear that I have found bits of carpet in the stair cupboard. How apt. They were behind the boxes of Carnation milk and sugar that Dad bought against famine. Do you remember when things were short in the shops a year or so ago? There was a spate of panic buying. Someone in Japan got crushed to death queuing for toilet rolls, and sugar was rationed for a spell here. Someone punched the manager at Cullen's.

———

Wash day again. Time flies. I will do fridge and disgusting oven in the morning. Must get another packet of bicarb.

———

Sophie has gone out to meet Beattie and was so late leaving she asked me to tell you she was sorry not to see you.

I was rather relieved. On her top half she was wearing a T-shirt in blotchy eau-de-nil and her denim pea jacket with the badges. Bottom half was sandals and a white cotton petticoat. She looked as if something frightful had happened when she was half dressed and she'd dropped everything and rushed out. I told her she might be a bit chilly from the waist down and she said she got an A in Art.

She has left three gnawed spare ribs on the kitchen table, which she had put in her bag at the restaurant last night to give to somebody's dog. I don't know whose dog. They weren't even her spare ribs.

———•———

Herewith:

- bottle of Gee's Linctus
- some Shield tablets

- wine gums
- Bourbon biscuits

Of course you can't hear anything – you've got cotton-wool in your ears.

Bit worried about Boot. Does she still meet you in the morning as usual? That strange third eyelid seems to be a bit stuck on her left eye.

Eleanor is much better. She rang me today. She is consumed with guilt about Mother's birthday. She sent a letter, and a parcel was to follow but her local PO was broken into the afternoon of the day she posted it. Men with guns. And it's a tiny place, she says. The sort that keeps dog biscuits in the window. The owner has shut up for a few days to recover. Eleanor says he looks awfully ill. Meanwhile the parcel is either still sitting there and the gunmen have got away with lavender talcum powder, some after-dinner mints and a tin of truffles.

———•—•———

I've found the keys. They were in the bottom of my wardrobe. Can you beat it? I had to sit down for a minute. What I think must have happened is that I hung up my cleaning holding the bunch of keys and let them go as all the hangers were put in place. Of course, the bottom of our wardrobe is full of shoes and scarves and old plastic bags and aprons so I didn't hear them fall. I might never have found them. But they're no use now and X pounds down the drain.

I am a dizzy tart. It runs in the family. Mother lost a pair of tights she'd bought in Dunoon and rang the shop fussing and furious only to find them in the fridge. There was one wet winter when she put her shoes to dry in the bottom oven of the Rayburn and forgot for weeks. Dinky little stone shoes they were.

No, I won't tell you how much. Put your pension to better use.

———•———

No, darling, I don't think there is any question of your having a cataract. I think that some of those library books have very small print, and the doctor feels the mistiness is to do with your general health, but we'll check at the op-thingummy.

You can see a cataract. My granny's was very noticeable.

I don't know why Aunt Min can't get hers done. Perhaps it's because of her diabetes? It's as simple nowadays as a tonsillectomy but I remember Granny's was a grand affair when you lay bandaged in a darkened room for ages. Of course, Granny refused. She got up immediately and wandered about the ward in her flannel nightie removing everyone's bandages as well as her own. In the end they sent her home for bad behaviour. Mother always says she got into an old gentleman's bed, but I don't think the old gentleman was there at the time.

We had to ban Granny as a subject of conversation because she was so appalling everyone wanted to know about her latest iniquity and other concerns were elbowed.

Do you know, she used to turn the electricity off at the mains if she felt people had overstayed their welcome. And when we had a visitor I would be sent upstairs to light the gas fire in their bedroom (the house was always freezing). When I'd done it I'd slide under the bed until I saw Granny's little black shoes tip-tapping to the fire to switch it off. Satisfied and breathing heavily, she would trot away to her room and I would emerge to relight the fire. She must have been ninety. My brother said she would live for ever because she ate all the mould off the top of the jam pots. My other job was to hide behind the curtains in the dining room to collect the dirty plates she carefully put away. She called it 'clean dirt' as she wiped them with a licked finger.

She put great faith in *spit*. I was about six when I fell heavily on a cinder path and a little cinder embedded itself in my forehead. Granny cleaned it up and spat on the wound. 'There now,' she said.

'That'll heal over nicely.' And it did. I had to go to the doctor's to have the cinder dug out. You can see the dent in my forehead to this day.

going to church

Around this time Gran had the first of her many falls. I found her on the loo floor with one little foot in its size-three shoe wedged around the lavatory pedestal. I couldn't pick her up because she was laughing so much. Eventually I managed to pull her into a sitting position and give her a cup of sweet tea.

'Oh, thank heaven I've *been*,' she said, hiccuping.

When I finally had her upright I walked her to her bedroom by placing her feet on my size fives, like you do with kids, and we swayed shrieking across the landing, counting loudly at each uncertain step.

This was when I learnt that severe bruising is more painful than a break, or so the doctor said. Bed rest was prescribed. We rigged up a commode on a dining chair with a Wedgewood tureen shaped like a cabbage beneath it. It sold at auction for quite a lot some time later.

Mother sends acres of healing love. She says she fell down the manse stairs with her portable wireless in one hand and her tea in the other so she knows how you feel.

Uncle Arthur is pretty well, considering. Ma got up the other morning very early and feeling chilly, only to find him kneeling at his open window and just wearing his pyjama jacket. She thought he was dead or praying but he was taking aim at a rabbit. He keeps a shotgun under his wardrobe. Mill's pet rabbit used to eat the sitting-room carpet. It had to have a hysterectomy and, appalled by its pain, she fed it port and Veganin. Killed it. She couldn't understand it because her monkey was an alcoholic. They all are, I'm told. When she took him to the pub, folk would ask what her little friend fancied. Port-and-brandy was his favourite.

The girls will serve tea in your boudoir at 4 p.m. or thereabouts. You are getting better, I can tell.

Matron

I got the Baby Bio. It's underneath the sink. Treated myself to a can of Leaf Shine (very expensive). The flipping tobacco plant I got from Molly gets me down. Can I rip off that yellow leaf now?

I've washed the fanlight at the front door and emptied the bluebottles out of the lampshade. What's more, I've given the door itself a coat of linseed oil because I found half a bottle in the hall cupboard. Used the paintbrush Dad ruined creosoting the deckchairs. Very successful. The linseed oil has softened the bristles. Also, which is good news, the holes in the panelling are not woodworm but marks from the drawing pins we used to put up the wreath at Christmas. Ha!

———·—·———

Mrs Wilson sends love. Her arthritis is being kept at bay with some injection or other. Do you fancy a go?

Mr Wilson fell down the tube-station stairs at Trafalgar Square last week and 'came to' in the Middlesex. He has a lump on his head the size of a cricket ball and the bruise is slipping down his face. Mrs W says he may have to have it lanced.

Dr P says you might think about getting up and sitting in your chair tomorrow afternoon.

The girls will re-open lessons with 'the Box'.

Normal service should resume on Monday.

Coming down the hill from the cleaners I saw Larry T on his front steps with a dustpan and brush, wearing yellow rubber Marigold gloves. He was about to clear up the corpse of a rat that had walked up the stairs, looked at him piteously and died on his doormat.

I had a friend who was having a bath when a rat came out of the loo, collected a bar of soap and went back down. She keeps the complete works of Shakespeare and a huge family Bible on the loo lid in between times. The rat apparently lived in the flat below where it ate a cardboard carton full of tampons, and built a brilliantly comfortable nest with the contents. They are clever creatures. Mr Richardson used to keep pet rats. They used to sit on his chest and nibble sugar off his moustache.

Shall I leave Boot in your room tonight?

Darling, do try not to worry about it. I'm sure that's part of the problem. Any sort of tension or trauma seems to seize one up. I can never go when I'm visiting. Think of Dad. He comes home from New Zealand to go to the loo. Release of tension, you see. Some people don't go for days together and it's quite normal. Queen Victoria was always writing to her children about constipation and fresh air. Then Albert died from bad drains. Ironic.

They did a lot of research on it during the war because of lifeboats. I mean people didn't go for three weeks or more. When you come to think of it, just a bucket on a boat. Maybe not even a bucket.

I think the Navy is an authority on constipation. It was a naval doctor who wrote that book on bran. Let's have another try. If I put it in soup it wouldn't make you cough. Or if I squidged it up with All-Bran, cream and sugar?

I don't want you to get like Uncle Arthur wandering about in his pyjama jacket eating Ex-Lax.

An Indian with a strong Welsh accent has just come to read the gas meter.

I put the bed mat on the lawn because I felt it couldn't stand being on the line while still wet. Some of the stitching is very rotten. It'll be an enormous task mending it, darling, but I'll bring the bag of bits and it'll be something to do while you are sitting.

Boot was sick again, but very neatly, and there was a little patch of fur in the middle so maybe the vet was right after all.

———•———

Sorry I didn't tell you about the dentist. I thought you looked a bit bleak when I got home. Forgot. Sorry. Of course, I was late leaving and I couldn't find my keys. (They were on top of the fridge.) Then I lost my handbag. (I'd put it down by the front door.) I didn't have time to come up.

I was running down Fawley Road when I noticed something odd about my left leg. A certain stiffness about the knee. I slowed down a bit and walked briskly on, thinking bleakly about old age. It wasn't till I was sitting on the tube that I noticed a dingy clump of cotton sticking out of my left trouser leg. I tried to pretend it was perfectly normal to pull a pair of knickers out of my trouser leg and push them into my handbag.

I once dropped my handbag on the tube whereupon it burst open and scattered a packet of Tampax all over the floor in front of a large class of small boys from that posh prep school in Hampstead.

Do you think we should manufacture a pocket on your pinny a little higher up? For the aid, I mean. When you sat down at lunch it was under the table. You'll have to bring it out and lay it down, trying always to have the little round speaker bit facing upwards – or outwards if it is clipped on to your pinny, and I think above waist level. ('Where is that?' you cry.) Up the 'orspital they said you might hear swishing noises from some materials you wear, and some fabrics crackle.

It worked best at tea, didn't it? I didn't raise my voice one little bit. If you sit there holding it towards me it works a treat. A carpeted room and no extraneous noise or fidgeting members of the public.

I don't think Sanatogen can make you dizzy. Were you bending down a lot? Looking at Boot? I know. I agree. There is a decided swelling.

Hurrah for Pooh.
For who? For Pooh!

Tremendous celebrations downstairs. Dad did a rather undignified dance from study to wine rack and will propose your health at supper tonight.

Sausages and mash.

I was so thrilled to see you beaming away all pink and pretty that I will not even impose sanctions on whoever smuggled in the Ex-Lax.

PS If I stew a large bowl of Bramleys to serve with the All-Bran, will you promise me not to take Ex-Lax every night?

Matron

He says it's cancer, darling, and he can't operate. I shall tell the girls at teatime. We'll probably come up to your room. Dad has gone to golf to stride about.

I went up to Flax's and bought a packet of smoked-salmon bits. He can't say how long she has left, but he gave her an injection of steroids and vitamins, which will give her a terrific boost and we should see a difference in her within twenty-four hours. She may even meet you tomorrow morning as of old, so take care on the landing.

She liked the smoked salmon.

See you at tea.

Well, onwards and upwards, darling. I may try and clean shed out tomorrow if weather continues fine. If not, I may do out china cupboard. I did floors very thoroughly last week, so if you do waist-level dusting, I'll just come behind you with the polisher.

waist level dusting.

Fish and chips takeaway? Haddock? Or, I know, what about *skate* if they have it? I'll just get one portion of chips and two of whatever we decide on because that will give us spare for Boot and batter for the birds.

———·———

I was sitting at the kitchen door in the last of the sun this evening doing the crossword when Boot came out and walked up to the end of the garden. The melancholy slowness of her walk struck me to the heart. She sat down, curled her tail round her body as neatly as ever she did and stared into the shadows. I put down my paper and called to her gently, and she turned and stared at me in an abstracted sort of way, and then when I held out my hand she moved towards me with the shadow of an old hope in her eyes, touched my hand with her dry hot nose and sat down on the crossword. That cheered me up.

Do you remember how we lost her not five minutes after we brought her to the house, and how wild with grief the children were and how even you wept till we found her in the cutlery drawer?

Do you remember how she used to live under our bed in order to occupy it when we left? Em used to call to her severely, 'Come out of there, Boot. I see your boiling eyes.'

Nor will I ever forget when she had her kittens in the bottom drawer of the wardrobe and I lay on the floor and held her hand. And Dad woke the RSPCA at two in the morning to tell them his cat was having a breech birth as all we could see were three tiny paws sticking out of her hindquarters.

And do you remember when we moved house I slept on a mattress in the sitting room to try and prevent her escaping up the chimney? Of course, that's when we discovered she could get out through the letter-box. So she was lost for two days and nights and we fed her poor children every two hours – or was it four? – with an eye-dropper. On the third night we heard her call in the garden and Dad fed the kittens outside so she slowly came nearer, tortured by their squeaks. After that she was fine.

I always wish I'd never had her 'doctored'. When she came home with that bandage round her middle, looking humiliated and aggrieved, I was stricken with guilt. She wouldn't look at me. There ought to be a pill they could take. Animals, I mean. Mother had a medical acquaintance who fed birth-control pills to pigeons to keep the numbers down.

Oh, Boot. We've never seen eye to eye, have we, till just these last weeks. What a successful, controversial cat you've been. I'm glad you were wicked and nicked Gran's fresh crab.

So there we sat in the sun and communed one with another and sighed over lost summer times.

Not surprisingly, I forgot the gingerbread so the edges are all black but the middle is surprisingly edible, if a bit chewy, so we just sat and ate it out of the tin. I'll have to soak the edges off.

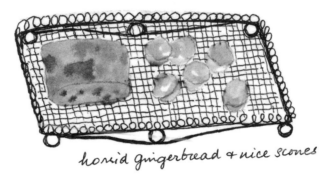

horrid gingerbread + nice scones

Your specs flew off and you landed on them so one of the legs is a bit bent. Dad has been trying to straighten them over the gas, but he's a bit tentative so I'll take them round to the oculist tomorrow.

But I'm amazed you didn't smash something. There's only a little chip on the hallstand and at least this time you weren't wearing two pairs of bloomers. Remember when you broke your leg in Scotland and you had put on two of absolutely everything for fireworks? That little Indian doctor had rather a testing time cutting you out of your drawers. He probably thought it was an ancient Scottish custom.

There is a bit of a bump on the side of your forehead, which will probably show up more tomorrow. You must have biffed your head on the banisters. Nurse thought you may get a black eye. Ooh. Gorgeous.

I'll just prop this up against the clock in case you wake. Take the yellow pill, darling.

Didn't they use to put a raw steak on a black eye? Why?

———————

Well done, Gran. You will find the yellow pill on spoon beside glass of soda water. Here are a few wine gums beside them. Hand bell by wireless. I've moved the flowers in case they get knocked over.

I'll ask Nursie about Benecol tomorrow. I know you have great faith in it but I think we'd better not take it till we know if it mixes with everything else.

I do wonder what it's made of. I simply cannot get it out of the carpet whatever I do, and I was scrubbing away the other day when I suddenly saw that the pattern on the edge has a line of helmeted warriors doing unmentionable things to each other. I had no idea it was so bellicose. Anyway, I've rubbed a couple of warriors threadbare and the Benecol is still clinging to the warp or the woof or the weft or whatever you call it – it's like paint.

Dad wants to know who is going to wash his knickers while his mum is confined to barracks. He chipped most of the gingerbread out of the tin and ate it. The mangled tin is soaking in the wash-house sink.

I enjoyed cleaning the stained-glass window. It's come up lovely so it has. I think the landing might seem brighter now, and the stair-rods are all fixed and firm. You know the rose you gave me from the Harrods flower show? The 'Pink Grootendorst' it's called, poor thing. Well, it's flourishing over on the other side of our fence, but it looks half dead this side. Rather hurtful. I saw this while hanging out of the window, so I sloshed all my soapy water over the bad bits and missed. Half the bucketful hit the deck and half went down that shiny new pipe sticking out of next door's side wall. I think I've flooded their central-heating system. When the doorbell went a while later I assumed it was next door come to complain. And there they were. I took a deep breath and started to apologize, but they'd only called to show us their new baby. Brought it up to see you but you'd dropped off. Nice little person no bigger than a thermos and very comfy in a carry-bag. I shut up about the central-heating. If I've wrecked it they'll only find out in September.

———

Mrs Wilson says she was nearly cremated this week. Mr Wilson filled her cigarette lighter too full, she says, and the flames shot up so high it set her spectacles on fire. She managed to throw them off but they were burning the carpet so she had to pick them up with fire tongs and put them in the sink. She says the smell was frightful.

I can't understand how her hair didn't catch fire. She uses masses of hair lacquer and it's very combustible.

'It's the absolute bitter end in whiskers,' she said.

Boot actually had a boxing match with Dad tonight.

He has put a cardboard box lined with a cushion and his copy of the Times by the kitchen heater.

———

Guess what? You will squeal. I got up this morning to investigate an odd sound. A cross between castanets and a kettle coming to the boil. I thought it was the central heating, so I felt the radiators in our room and thought, That's it. They're tepid at the top so they probably need milking or bleeding or whatever it's called. Wandered to the bathroom and the noise followed me onto the landing. Went to the loo and it stopped. It got very loud suddenly when I went near the laundry basket so I emptied it out in case there was something lurking in a pocket. Nothing.

(Well, one ½d bit.) Opened my drawer to get some clean knickers and while I was struggling them on the noise got rather aggressive. Sat on the bed nonplussed and scratched my head. There it was. There it was. The noise, I mean, the rattling about. I'd run out of curlers last night and I'd used a tube of Anadin with six pills in it on my fringe and jammed it into place with two bent hairpins. It's done the trick with the curl, I think you'll find.

PS Do you remember the night I swallowed my moustache bleach?

———·—·———

Went to get our Friday fish this afternoon and told our bespectacled friend about Boot. He had wondered about all that smoked salmon. Goodness, he is nice. I think you might have to be nice to be a fishmonger. Carpenters are nice. Do they start nice or is it the job? Anyway, Spectacles was the one who said to drown your crab. I thought this sounded idiotic but he said, 'No. Drop it upside down into warm water and wait till it stops bubbling.' Help. It's time you were up. If the water is too hot he says the crab will 'shoot its claws' (as in gents shooting their shirt cuffs). He and his wife are very keen on amateur theatricals and he was a virgin when he married. I didn't enquire about his wife.

My uncle Charlie announced one New Year's Eve that he was a virgin. You should have heard the aunts. They shrieked. He wasn't a proper uncle or they would have known. Not quite sure how he got to be uncled. Anyway, he was a private in World War I and in his first week at the front he dropped his rifle in the mud and ruined it. His commanding officer shouted a lot and he was ordered to steal one from the next dug-out, which he did. And then he sat about for so long in the mud that the seat of his trousers rotted, so he stuck a tin biscuit lid inside them for protection. 'I always took it out on fine days,' he said, 'in case it caught the sun and a sniper took aim.'

Father said that the Cameron Highlanders were ordered to muddy their spats because they were a dazzling white target for the Hun. Within 24 hours the order was countermanded by the Big Chief Cameron of Lochiel who presumably didn't want his Highlanders to look slovenly when dead.

But I digress. Poor young Charlie came a cropper on his first bombardment. It was what he called a whizz-bang bomb, which sounds rather fun but wasn't. You had to judge the direction it was coming from and he ran the wrong way.

I think he lost his crown jewels, the whole arrangement. His voice stayed deep enough but it hardly compensates.

———————

Glad you liked the pudding. We made it with 'foozle'. This was my granny's favourite. You boil a tin of Carnation milk – not condensed, Carnation. I think for about ten minutes or so. At least until the label comes off. Then it whizzes up into a dropping-cream consistency.

I remember watching horrified as Granny poured it over her salad. I dared not utter. She ate it with relish and declared it delicious. I think she had it with

"Foozle"

her pudding as well. We all used to leave the disgusting cooking sherry at the bottom of the trifle Flora made and Granny would polish it off. She never would have done so had she known it was the demon alcohol. She always poured every dreg in bottle or glass into the rose-bowl on the dining table.

Someone who shall be nameless has put bubble gum on the dresser and lifted the veneer.

Bit of an atmosphere downstairs.

Ta-ra!

Darling, I can't believe you heard them! It was two hedgehogs. Dad put out a tin plate of bread and milk when he saw the first one. I told him milk was bad for them but he didn't believe me. Nor would the hedgehogs. When the second one turned up there was an ugly scene, followed by vigorous sex on the tin plate. Imagine. All those prickles. How do they manage? We were agog. I do hope it was a successful union.

Sex on a tin plate

Now it's raining and Dad has given them his golf umbrella.

———•———

This will make you shriek. Mrs Wilson made little portions of chicken chasseur in plastic pots neatly sealed with clingfilm and put them in the deep freeze for Mr Wilson whilst she was away in 'orspital for her cataract operation.

Mr Wilson just put them in the oven as they were and ate the lot – pots and all. He's rather ill.

Not sure what it is, Gran. I think the chasseur bit is a cream sauce of some sort. Not your scene, I know.

———•———

Well, it's tragic downstairs. Boot is to go to the vet tomorrow. She will get an injection and he says she will just slip away. Em will take her, she wants to. Oh dear.

The banging you heard this evening was Dad

removing the cat flap and boarding the hole up against the draught. He waited tactfully till Soph had gone out, which was quite funny as she scoured all Boot's dishes and hid them behind the shed while *he* was out. She is to plant them up, she says.

There will be a short ceremony in the garden at a later date. You will be advised.

It seems there is a new deaf-aid on the market. I keep seeing it. It's like an Alice band so you wear it on your head with these wee muff things that sit on your ears. Very practical. You'd be surprised how many young people are wearing them. You are not alone. I shall do a bit of research and report back, because I think they might be the very thing.

———·—·———

Darling, please don't worry. I'm sure it's just the bruising. Nursie said it was very severe. You were X-rayed upside down and sideways so they would be bound to see if the joint was loose. It's a big thing, like a light bulb and I think it's made of stainless steel.

Your specs are looking as good as new. The optician says they were all squinty and he thinks you've been taking them off by one leg. He says lift them off carefully in the middle on the bridge of your nose, or with both hands. Do you see what he means? He didn't charge by the way. Nice man. Says he'll come round to see you and maybe devise a padding for the specs so they won't clank about on your hearing-aid.

Talking of which! I told Dad about the new deaf-aid on the market and he tells me it's a thing called a Walkman which plays music into your ears. He and the girls were hysterical. Trust me to get it wrong!

———

It's a 'Zimmer', darling. A 'zither' is a musical instrument. Could come in useful for airing things, Dad says. Give it a go. It's a help to get to the loo at least, and awfully useful for getting out of bed if I leave it just beside you, pointing in the right direction. You can really lean on it. I do see that your mattress is a bit squashy and difficult to lift off. I wonder if we could put a board under it? My old drawing board might do. We'll try it.

Your black eye has gone a lovely yellow colour now with a tasteful purple swelling near your nose. Can you see? I expect it will slip downwards shortly since you are sitting up so much more. Very attractive. Mother always keeps 2 cotton-wool pads soaked in witch hazel on the top shelf of the fridge and recommends old cold teabags and slices of cucumber, but I don't think we can cope with such frippery. You hate the smell of witch hazel too, I seem to remember.

———•———

What made you think of Xmas? Good grief. Don't worry for the moment. I suspect we'll spend it at home this year anyway. I'd love to go up for New Year and you might be ready for the Dashing White Sergeant by then. You and Uncle Arthur. Can't you see it?

Actually, he used to be a bit of a lounge lizard.

All those medals he keeps were for ballroom dancing, in particular the foxtrot, the two-step and the tango. (What is the two-step, by the way?) He would gallantly take me on to the floor at New Year celebrations and I'd be clamped firmly to his chest and his down below bits, which made me shriek and I always got calamine lotion over his suit. My back was covered in acne and Mother would try and cover it up, as my dance frock was a ghastly floral creation with a bathing-costume top made of stretchy elastic. Uncle Arthur would plonk his hot hand on my back and leave a full imprint. Oh, the shame!

Nor could I ever remember the moves in the eightsome reel, so Uncle Arthur would yank me around and everyone else would shout insults. Isn't growing up ghastly?

I loved New Year in Glasgow when I was home from school, especially when old Mrs Keith came. She was a tiny little person, terribly crippled by

Three Mothers (and a camel)

Mrs Keith

arthritis, and we adored her. She sat by the fire in the sitting room for all her meals and we would beg to be allowed to serve her. Best was to take in her tiny glass of sloe gin, which she held in her little paws so gently to sip, and under her skirts were huge black-patent pumps with a flat grosgrain-ribbon bow. Her wee feet were so bumpy and bent her shoes had to be big as boats. She was out of Dickens, really. I have very dim memories of old Mr Keith who was a little hunchback of a sweet soul with a huge red nose like Mr Punch. He used to keep a warehouse by the docks in Greenock or Paisley or somewhere, and they always had donkeys, parakeets, monkeys and other strange animals sent from abroad. I can't tell you why. I seem to think they were in quarantine. Mother said some bizarre foreign bird arrived at the warehouse and started to moult, and of course being winter by the docks, it would be damp and cold so little Mrs Keith knitted it a sort of woollen body stocking. She made herself little woollen mittens and turned heels and all such. Bad for the arthritis is knitting I'm told, so beware.

bizarre foreign bird

Mending our patchwork quilt would be all right tho', wouldn't it? Hint. Hint.

Well, we went to Scotland for New Year. Of course we did. We took the patchwork with us. Our journey was meticulously planned. We rose early and Gran took no tea. The glove compartment was closely packed with egg sandwiches, Maynard's wine gums, several bananas, one orange and any milk left in the fridge.

Forton was our favoured stop on the M6. We ignored the bridge café and drove straight to the petrol station, which had a loo with a ramp easily negotiable on a zimmer frame. When Gran was comfortably returned to the car, she would give me some of her pension to buy my coffee, chocolate raisins and liquorice allsorts for pudding.

In our first years together things had been very different. We went by sleeper on the Royal Scot, smuggling Boot, then a kitten, into our carriage where she slept on my face. In later years she was weighed on the platform and given a ticket. Mostly she travelled with us in the car and threw up, howling, at Stafford.

The train was a triumph. The ferry crossing was a nightmare. To Gran, it was sheer insanity to travel on water. Long years before, her first sweet-heart had gone to Canada to seek his fortune and sent her a ticket so that she could join him. She refused. She couldn't face the ocean crossing. Her father went instead. I got the impression that he did rather well, but when he was travelling home, in steerage, the weather was fierce. He caught bronchitis, kept it, and died.

So started Gran's long life in service, often in and around London for I know she saw Zeppelins during World War 1. They came over on moonlit nights and seemed so low she felt she could put out her hand and touch them.

Then she was a cook in a country hotel where she fell in love with the waiter – there was only one. Every Friday she cooked an omelette for a gentleman who called on his motorbike. It was T. E. Lawrence. She called him Mr Ross. 'He loved my omelettes,' she said.

On that very first ferry crossing, it was only the rumour of a school of dolphins that persuaded Gran to open her eyes, squeezed tight shut against drowning. By a rare miracle the water was satin smooth. She didn't see the dolphins. She saw the hills.

And then she saw the cottage. Her old rose, 'New Dawn', was overwhelming the tiny porch, creeping under the gutters and shifting the slates.

Everything enchanted her, even the weather – even the outside loo. We all spent too long in there, with the door open wide to the view: a local seal spent early mornings perched on a flat rock, like a slice of melon.

Milk was delivered daily in a can by the gate and smelt of cows. Gran liked to fetch the *Sunday Post* herself from the tiny post office next door and chat to Mrs Gardener, the postmaster's wife, who played the violin on Burns night with her back to the audience.

And then there was Gertie Mackay who sat at her door on a lobster pot and waylaid Gran on her way to the village tea rooms and fresh pancakes. They shared stories about their life in service. In Gertie's day it had been customary to clean the house mercilessly for Hogmanay. 'Seven washing waters and vinegar in the final rinse,' said Gertie.

The kids would fill pails with mussels and winkles from the shore and Dad would catch buckets of mackerel, bringing them home on a string for Gran to gut and fry. Once he got a fish hook embedded in his hand and fainted. 'He doesn't get that from me,' she said.

For serious shopping we went to 'town', stocking up on essentials like potato scones, mutton pies and 'squashed-fly cemeteries', a particularly appealing fruit slice. In summer there was rhubarb ice-cream, and in winter the best fish and chips on the coast. 'Town' was Dunoon, voted the 'top resort in Scotland'.

A decent whisky and top snacks were always kept for first-footers at Hogmanay but this time we didn't go to the fireworks. Not in the dark on a zimmer frame. Some years before we had set out for the party on a frosty night when the sky was crusty with stars but no moon. We had just waltzed down the path to the little gate, from which steps led to the road, when I ran back to fetch a decent torch and Gran, launching herself into the darkness, fell onto the road and broke her thigh. That was when the young Indian doctor had to cut her out of her double bloomers.

I was only too pleased to use Gran as an excuse to go to bed with lights out before the dreaded midnight hour when ships hooted at each other on the Clyde.

New Year's Eve supper had been classic. Mother had made a creamy rice mould for one pudding, decorated with grated pistachio nuts. With a mouthful of ham, Uncle Arthur suddenly shouted: 'That pudding is moving!' The pistachios were walking about. Mother had kept them for years and they were full of weevils. Sophie says Mother's fridge is like a scientist's laboratory.

The cold and damp always affected what Gran would call her 'war wounds'. She used to say she had discovered Scotland too late and quite often came to breakfast saying she had been wandering the hills all night. On one of our early summers we took her up the hill we called 'Boiled Egg Bump', since it was perfect for picnics. She just had a bit of difficulty coming down.

'It's the same on Everest,' Dad said.

Lately, and unsurprisingly, the war wounds had troubled Gran more than usual. One doctor thought she might have broken a rib sneezing. But she hadn't sneezed. On our long, wistful journey home she was quiet and uncomplaining but it was clear that it pained her very much coming out of what she called her 'stuck sitting' position.

I was concerned. Safely upright and on her zimmer frame she said of the pain: 'It'll go the way it came.'

Apologies, darling, for such a late cuppa. I locked myself OUT. My keys were in my jacket pocket and I'd just shoved my coat on over my nightie to go to Mistry's and get some milk. (The kids made cocoa last night.) Climbed over the back gate with great difficulty. Made a pile of those bricks left over from the front path and that gave me a boost. Hoisted me and milk up and sat astride the gate rather painfully, plucking up courage to throw myself into the yard, having tossed the milk into that lavender bush by the water butt. Slid down the back door ripping nightie on the bolt and hoping against hope that the kitchen door might be open. It wasn't. Peered in all the windows in the faint hope of help. Sat on the back step and swigged some milk miserably.

Then I remembered the plot of a rather famous French film called 'Rififi' or something, where robbers used an umbrella to catch a key. I just used a sheet of your Daily Mail I found in the dustbin. I pushed this under the door below the keyhole. Then I found, after much fossicking, a peculiarly strong twig, which I pushed into the keyhole, wiggling it about to dislodge the key, which I could just see by leaning against the door and squinting thru the glass. It took ages but, to my joy, the key finally dropped on to the paper, which I tenderly withdrew and, lo!, I unlocked the door and put the kettle on. Rather damp, scratched and torn, with a button off my coat (yes, please), but what a TRIUMPH.

Do you remember that nice policeman who got into my Volkswagen Beetle with a coat-hanger? He wouldn't let me watch.

———•———

I don't know if they cremate cats. I should have asked. Do you think we'd get her ashes in a tiny urn? I've kept her flea collars and her bell.

There was a chap in Ma's village called Gully Wishart who had so many cats he wore flea collars on his wellingtons.

We'll have Boot's short memorial service soon and plant something. Cat mint? Does it repel or attract? I've never known.

Mrs Wilson has asked to be scattered along the

path she takes to the tennis courts. Arnold says his uncle Clem wanted to have his ashes scattered off Blackpool pier, but Auntie Blanche thought they would get blown back all over people so she only took his teeth. Even that was a bit dodgy, she said.

Wait till you hear this. Mother had Miss Delmahoy to tea. Do you remember her? She used to be Matron at a big hospital in Glasgow and she has retired to a bungalow across the way next door to Mrs Moffat. It is she who has that fantastic garden, and Mother is desperate to pick her brains. Mrs M says Miss D gardens with a big silver-plated serving spoon and tells stories of the amount of cardboard coffins she had to order and store for World War II. She's known besides for doing intricate tapestry work called Richelieu, using fine black and gold thread, and she keeps it on a frame like a music stand, covered in muslin when she isn't working on it, rather like old Queen Mary waiting for her carriage. She used to make stair-carpets, Queen Mary did. I once saw an example displayed at the English Speaking Union in Berkeley Square. Bet she had help.

Well, anyway, Ma was determined to do things properly so she unpacked the tea-set from the dining-room dresser and washed it tenderly, checking everything for chips in case of GERMS. She even bleached the inside of the teapot with a touch of Domestos. She got a large carton of whipping cream from Ross's Dairies in Dunoon to serve with fresh scones and this year's bramble jelly. Perfect. Miss D duly arrived. She always ignores the bell, knocks peremptorily (is that a word?) and walks straight in. Then it transpired that she takes lemon in her tea so there was a bit of a kerfuffle while Ma looked for a lemon and could only find half of a rather old squashed one in the fridge, and then she couldn't concentrate on anything because she was sure the tea tasted of bleach. Miss D talked all the time, which made it easier. It was only after they had toured the garden and Miss D had departed that Ma found her tea-plate with her napkin delicately covering most of her uneaten scone. Ma had been in such a flap that she had taken the wrong carton out of the fridge and served the warmed scone with cottage cheese instead of Jersey cream.

Uncle Arthur said the tea was disgusting. Ma says there's no way she'll sleep tonight.

———————

Gran, it's remarkable. I've never seen your skin so clear. You must be thrilled. D'you think it's because of this enforced rest? Posh people with psoriasis spend pots of money and rush off to the Dead Sea, which sounds alarming, but I understand bathing in its salty water is very efficacious. I'd have thought it was agony getting salt into those raw patches, but it's bordering on miraculous and apparently you can float on the surface reading a newspaper. Something to do with the salt. You simply can't sink. The Adriatic is pretty salty. I couldn't get my bottom under the water. Dad said it looked as if I was being followed by a baby elephant. Or a small island.

You are still taking the gloop, aren't you? Or did we stop it? Whatever. I think it's the total rest. But while you are sitting up for lunch or tea, please remember to waggle your ankles, toes pointing up!

baby elephant?

Toes pointing down! And then round and round as demonstrated by Nursie. Life is not all beer and skittles.

Matron

———

Where's your clean nightie, Gran? He's coming to see you tomorrow after surgery. When I told him there was this blobby thing next to your sternum (posh name for your breastbone) he was thrilled and asked if I was a nurse. Maybe even a doctor? I said, no, but I was sure I could deal with the blob very neatly before tea. It's just like an ounce of suet, I said, no bigger than a baby's bootee and just under the skin. A quick snip and that's that. He said perhaps not. Ooh, I'd love to do it. It wouldn't take a minute and, after all, I had my tonsils taken out on the dining-room table.

It's not a generally known fact but I did intend to become a doctor. Don't laugh. Do you remember during the war there were huge posters warning people about VD? In Glasgow they were everywhere. Aunt May said it meant Digging for Victory but I could read the small print. Besides, they were on the back of every public loo door so that you could read all the details from a perched position. I made undercover enquiries in a luridly illustrated medical dictionary I found in Granny's bookshelves only to discover that I had all the symptoms listed and would surely die young and in disgrace. My best friend Isobel Hebblethwaite said you could catch it from loo seats so when I stayed with her I used to pee in the sink. Realising I was socially unacceptable, the obvious career move was to sacrifice myself for the human race and maybe work with lepers in the Gorbals.

Oops, there's the phone.

That was Mother. Everything much as usual. Yesterday she found Uncle Arthur buttoned and belted into his raincoat. Lying on the sofa head back, mouth open, specs squint, teeth dangling. She thought he was dead and went to phone the surgery. Just as the doctor answered Uncle Arthur shouted, "He owes me £1."

she thought he was dead

I think the doctor is the only well-dressed man ever to darken our door. He even wears a waistcoat. Thank God we tidied your bedroom. Of course, when he rang the doorbell I was creaming butter and sugar with that electric whizzer thing you gave me and the bell startled me so that I lifted it out of the bowl without turning it off and covered the walls with gobbets of cake mix. Typical. I thought he was coming after *evening* surgery.

Anyway, he seemed delighted to view the baby's bootee and not unduly worried about anything except what he describes as your "pallor". What does he expect? It's not much fun baring your bosom to young men in mid-morning. However, he will be in touch shortly as he is going to send us to a friend of his in the 'orspital who, he says, is top man for bumps and awfully nice. He will make the appointment, he says, and hopes to let us know within the week. Huh, we'll see.

I'm off to put the kettle on and clear the kitchen. Back with cuppa shortly. Well done, Gran. You were brilliant.

Dixon of Dock green
or
This is Your Life

PS Can we watch the snooker up here with you tonight?

———————

Just in case we get called to the hospital within a week or so, let's get your hair done. Tracey can come on Thursday, and backwards over the sink is all right now, isn't it? I'll bring up that kitchen chair.

I think your best blouse is in the laundry bag still. I'll wash it today. Don't laugh. I will, and I'll hang out the tweed pinny with the zip. You don't want to have to pull anything over your head. Actually, your stays will be difficult for a doctor to negotiate. Can you use garters for your stockings? We'll take a wheelie for the endless corridors and you'll be sitting down for the viewing. Maybe your bloomers will keep your stockings up, if you are sitting down. That's if the elastic is tight enough.

Reminds me of old Mrs Hatrick up the glen who had a thing about spiders. She says she saw their teethmarks in the butter and used elastic bands to tighten the legs of her bloomers because she thought spiders would invade.

Remember Boot eating spiders and throwing up over your bedcover? We will discuss and unravel the garter problem tonight.

———

My drawing board is under your mattress, so can we bring the old card table into your room? The aim is to finish the jigsaw before you go in for the boob job. It might be quite fun and any visitor can wander in and add a piece here and there. Dad says if we rearrange the furniture a bit we can get it all set up under the window and you can have your chair beside it. Hurrah.

———

Gran's room had always been a storeroom with a bed in it. She welcomed this sort of interference and she loved it when we watched the snooker lying on her bed, the only available space in the room other than her big armchair. In its heyday Gran's cottage must have had elastic sides. It was home for one husband for a bit, three sons, one daughter, an elderly mother, an elderly dog and, during the war, a floating population of evacuees. Anything that interfered with the general flow was thrown higgledy-piggledy into Gran's little bedroom at the top of the narrow stairs. Problem solved.

After the war, things thinned out. One by one the boys left home and eventually she shared the cottage with her daughter, her daughter's husband and their small son, who was the apple of Gran's eye. We used to take our girls to stay or just visit for treat weekends. I remember with awe the massive teas served on a spotless lace-edged tablecloth. The children, their noses level with the table top and eyes on the cake, equally awed, behaved like angels. No, not the jam tarts quite yet. Bread and butter first. There was always a bag of Mixed Assortment to be handed round when we watched Gran's favourite *Dixon of Dock Green* in the front room.

Then one summer Gran was due into London from a visit to her eldest son who lived abroad, and I was to put her on the train home to Horsham. I think I was washing up when the phone went. It was her son-in-law ringing from the cottage. 'Is she there?' he asked.

'No! She isn't expected till three fifteen,' I said.

'My wife,' he said. 'The drawers are empty and the wardrobe is full of hangers.'

Gran's daughter had run away to Cornwall with a beautiful young man, taking her little son with her.

I made up a bed and a thermos of hot, sweet tea. I told Gran in the car that I was going to take her home to our place at least for a night and I told her why. She took the news, mug in hand, with surprising equanimity. I drank most of the tea.

Years later, I learnt that Gran had helped pack up her daughter's clothes for her flight. Not many moons later she packed up her own and came to us.

———•———

It occurs to me that we ought to cut your nails before D-Day. I don't think they do that sort of thing in 'orspital. You can soak your feet while jigging and sawing and we'll use Dad's clippers.

Let's watch Delia Smith tonight?

———

We've lost the lid of the jigsaw, so we will have to struggle without looking at the picture. It's not so much the ship, it's all that blue of sky and sea.

———

I've checked the elastic in your bloomers and I think they'll be fine. It was Granny who used to wear wee garters of black elastic on her enormous knee-length bloomers. They were an unfortunate green, which seemed to glow in the dark. When she went walk-about guests were horrified to be confronted by a small bald ghost wearing plus-fours. She left her bunch of false curls on the dressing-table after nine at night when she was on patrol before bed and on

unfortunate green bloomers

her way to turn the electricity off at the mains. She said she had a degree in electricity. Her gnashers were kept in a bedside jug, tho' quite often they rattled about in her bed-jacket pockets among 'sneesh paper' and charcoal biscuits. She left a trail everywhere she went like Hansel and Gretel and me with hairpins.

———·—

Yes, I know, I'm frightful about Granny but she was such a thundering old bigot. If nuns called collecting, we all rushed to the door before Granny, as she was a miniature version of Ian Paisley and quite as loud. Once she had shouted about the Pope being an instrument of the devil, she would play wobbly hymns on the piano and sing off-key in an uncertain soprano.

I did enjoy sitting with her in 'the morning room' when she read the paper breathing heavily and peering thru a large magnifying glass. With any luck you might get a bit of chocolate from her bureau drawer. She would prise out the soft centre with one of her hairpins, eat it, return the hairpin to her bun, and hand me the chocolate shell. Sometimes she gave me the Russian Toffee because that stuck to her dentures, but I found her careful concentration and her clicking teeth rather soothing.

PS My specs were found under the washing line when I stepped on them. They must have fallen off when I pinned up your blouse.

———

Mother sends much love. She is fed up. Uncle Arthur has been very mumpish. Mrs Mac sent round some lovely home-baked ham studded with cloves and he complained bitterly that 'Mrs Mac might be all very well, but her ham was full of nails.'

He won't eat Ma's mashed potato either and asked for the stuff in a packet called Smash. 'No lumps,' he said.

———

Talking of which, there is movement on the lump front. We are to go on Friday next at 11.15 a.m., which is wonderfully much sooner than expected tho' I don't like the look of that '15' detail. Can he be seeing people every 15 minutes? We'll take the Daily Mail, a pen and some wine gums. Thank Heaven we got your hair done.

It'll be nice to get it over before next weekend when we are all at home and a roast is planned. You may be allowed to recline with Room Service on Saturday and then you will be escorted downstairs to oversee the Yorkshire pudding department. What do I do wrong? Dad stuck my last efforts to the fridge door and is demanding 'the nun's farts' his mother makes.

—·—

Ooh, what about that surgeon? Wasn't he gorgeous? Long time since I've seen a bow tie. When he bent to pat you on your shoulder I thought he was going to kiss you.

'Half man, half woman,' he murmured admiringly.

I told him you had that boob off forty years ago and he was THRILLED. He said you were 'a miracle'.

Did you mind all those students having a feel? I was a bit worried and the surgeon said rather firmly they weren't to *squeeze* it. In medical terms it's known as a Mouse apparently.

Do you mind nurses calling you Annie? I felt you might.

Anyway, Mouse is to be removed and Mr McClure, the surgeon, is looking forward to it. All very well for him, I say, but he makes it sound easy and comfortably imminent.

———•—•———

I know tea was a bit peculiar, Gran, but Sophie was determined to impress. It's called Lamb Moroccaine or something. I can't explain why it was grey but the fingernails were actually flaked almonds. I shall waltz in later with your Sanatogen and the last of the cake.

———•—•———

Don't worry, Gran, we've got time, but let's make a list tomorrow. Where's your wee case? It used to be on top of the wardrobe. Lost? Talking of which – Mother couldn't find Uncle Arthur this morning when she took him his tea. He'd got into bed upside down. His head was where his feet should be if you follow me.

———

We'll use some of this baby talc to stop your legs sticking together.

I'll turn your radiator off in your room. It's horrid getting hot and sweaty because it makes you cold. Aunt Ella sweated so much at night she took a hair dryer to bed with her. She said it had nothing to do with the weather.

———

Right. Paper and pen at the ready. Let's make a list of requirements.

- talcum powder
- paper hankies
- 2 *good* hankies for handbag and pocket
- 2 nighties? One on and I bring a clean when needed?
- dressing-gown
- your sponge bag with –
  soap, facecloth, hairbrush and comb
- Steradent
- big tub psoriasis cream
- bottle of arthritis gloop
- those yellow pills
- handbag with purse with coins in for buying newspaper etc.
- Daily Mail
- pen and pencils
- book – I got you a Reginald Arkell at the library
- two pairs of specs and, last but not least, your hearing-aid. We might get help with that while you are in.
- Please tick list and add any other requirements.

Quite agree – I think Maynards wine gums essential. Well done.

———•———

Mother says she has discovered why the prize fuchsia overwinters so well. You will recall I know that Uncle Arthur won a prize for it at last year's flower show having bought it the day before at Marks & Spencer or was it Woolworths? Anyway, he has it in its pot just below the bedroom window and she caught him peeing on it.

Shades of the aunts, three of whom sat backwards out of an upstairs window and peed on a parishioner's flowery hat while she sat talking to their papa. I loved that story when I was little and even now I wish I'd known my grandpapa. He died rather young, and not surprising after Granny and eight children. Mother's memories of him are rare, but he used always to wear a velvet smoking jacket when he was at home, and if she cried in the night and he came to sit on her bed, she knew she would find a stick of nougat in his breast pocket.

I was about 9 when I got caught short in the ladies' compartment of the little local train to Wemyss Bay and boarding school. The train was

Three Mothers (and a camel)

he peed on his first prize

corridor-less and loo-less, so I ate all the choco-
lates from a Christmas gift box, peed into it and
threw the box out of the window just past Fort
Matilda.

———•———

Your case was under the bed.

Dad has ascertained that wheelchairs are always
available and he polished your shoes before he left.

No, darling. Manchester.

We'll cab it to the hospital as Dad has got
the car.

In Manchester.

He has added a packet of Rich Tea biscuits to
your luggage.

Your carriage is ordered for 10 a.m.

No, darling, he's in Manchester.

We will be very leisurely, and you won't be
harassed by anyone. Mr McClure will visit you
perhaps, but he's nice. Your case is packed and
ready, outdoor clothing hanging up neatly by the
airing cupboard.

You've got your nightie on back to front. That's tremendously good luck. Did you know?

————·—————

The tall one in dark blue with the wee hat is a big sister. I think there aren't any Matrons any more. (She's very young, isn't she?) The pretty wee blonde in the pink stripes with the frilly hat is from Great Ormond Street and visiting or something. I miss all those daft wee organdie hats nurses used to wear. The staff nurses here look like hairdressers or checkout girls from Sainsburys.

The dark girl with bottle-top specs wearing a white coat is American or Canadian, I think, and very keen to interview you when you are available. She's doing a 'paper' or a dissertation or some such and she is fascinated by your interesting condition. One boob and a bump.

Don't know who is behind the curtains next door. No, it's not a man.

The young women opposite are a bit yellow, which is jaundice, I think. We both look very large and pink.

Am just disappearing to the loo for a minute. I can't go into the ward one. It's over there.

It wasn't far. Just outside the ward doors. Sister says you'll be done first in the morning. Expect to be wheeled off around 8 a.m. I forgot it's nil by mouth. There's a large notice behind your head.

I'm glad you get done first. You'll be back up by lunchtime and I'll be here about 3 p.m. to eat your grapes. You are a pretty sight sitting there. The nurses are mad about you already.

OK, sweetheart, I'm off. We shall take tea tomorrow together. I've just seen a trolley waltzing about.

Got everything?

Nurse has your medicaments.

Wine gums on your locker. Better ask if they're allowed.

They'll probably give you a pill to sleep. I hope so. It's a bit noisy behind the curtain.

No, it's a woman. The man is just visiting. Ta-ta.

Gran! I've left a wee notebook and a pen on your locker for nurses to write things in case you don't hear them.

3.05 p.m. You are asleep, Gran! I'll be back later.

I've brought your post, Gran. It's like Christmas. Can't read this one. Who is Piggy? Your specs are in your handbag. Shall we do this later? I'll put them out on your locker. Don't think about it now.

I've started on your room. Found a desiccated sock behind the radiator.

I took your clothes home yesterday and I'll bring you a clean nightie when needed. You are wearing a hospital gownie. The yellow ladies are looking better. How is the curtained lady?

Oh.

Isn't it quiet at the weekend? There will be no action till Monday. Is it painful just now, Gran? I'll tell Nursie. She'll want to know.

Will you eat any of this?

Let's ask for a cuppa and you can dunk a Rich Tea. I'll ask too if you can have a hot milk drink tonight. Horlicks or Ovaltine. Not chocolate. OK

I'll just give your specs a clean. Where's your

hearing-aid? The family are coming up from Sussex to see you tomorrow so you will need it.

Gran, look. See this? It's your Visitor's Book. Get them to write in it.

It's absolutely pelting out there. I think I'll just get in beside you.

No, I came by cab. Dad has the car in Manchester.

You are tired. I'm going to go! I won't come tomorrow as everyone else is calling in. See you Monday. Not Dad. He's in Manchester. I'll see Sister before I go.

TTFN.

———•———

Ooh, get you, Annie Amelia. Tuppence to talk to you.

Big Sister and no less than three gorgeous doctors discussing your case across your bed. Could you hear what they were saying?

I longed to join in. They've all walked off looking important.

I've brought your post.

Your specs are on your nose.

I'll read the Visitors' Book.

You are to get an extra special X-ray tomorrow. They are concerned about your arthritis in the spine and it would be good to get that sorted while you're here. They aren't interested in your ears.

Sister says you are lovely. She'd like to keep you. Sounds as if you'll be coming home soon.

Yip. Yip.

Great excitement at home. Your room looks gorgeous already.

Sister says they'll send you home by ambulance and the hospital will loan us a bed-board and a monkey wrench.

That can't be right. No. Not a wrench. That's a tool of some sort, isn't it? No, this is something you can hang onto to lift yourself to a sitting position. The girls are particularly entranced by the scaffolding round the loo. It's spectacular. The loo is now a throne room.

Handles everywhere and a new battery in your wireless.

We won't all be at home when you get back, but I think that's quite good. It's always exhausting to travel and you need a few nights' good sleep. You will get a visit from Dr Thingummy and a nurse is to call to put on a new dressing.

Tunnocks Caramel Wafers are from Em and the Snowballs are from Soph. You'll be sick.

They gave her a year. She had a week. Almost her last words to me were 'I won't have any fish and chips tonight, darling.'

It was a Friday.

All things considered I'd rather be in DUNOON

How Many
Camels
Are There
in
Holland?

Dementia, ma and me

For my daughters and the Golden Girls

What is your full name?
How old are you?
When were you born?
What year is this?
What month is this?
What day of the week is this?
What date is this?
What is the name of this place?
What town/city are you in?
What is your mother's maiden name?
Who is the current PM?
Who was the PM before him?
Without looking at the clock what time is it?
Are you right-handed or left-handed?
Say the names of the months forwards
(January to December). Now backwards.
Count backwards in 7s from 100.

Brief Cognitive Status Exam

IN THE BEGINNING

My mother, Meg, was the seventh of eight children and the youngest of five sisters born to a Presbyterian minister and his tiny indomitable wife, who lived to terrorise us all.

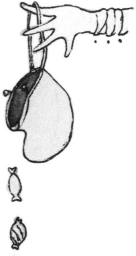

Mother remembered very little about her papa, except that he wore a velvet smoking jacket of an evening and kept a bar of nougat in his breast pocket for little fingers to find. They had sweets only on Sunday when they spent the day in church, eating lunch and tea in the vestry, after which sweets would be found on the church floor, dropped accidentally-on-purpose from velvet reticules by little old ladies.

Papa died young. Grannie went into mourning and took her eight children to Australia, where her brother was a professor at the University in Sydney. Mother was still wearing woollen hand-me-downs. When Grannie became ill the doctor advised a return to a cooler climate. The children were perfectly willing. Ripe mangoes were nice, but locusts were nasty. They took the boat home in 1913. Grannie said there were spies on board, and her beautiful Titian-haired daughters caused havoc among the crew. Aunt Mary got engaged to a sailor, who went down with Kitchener in 1916.

Back in Glasgow, in reduced circumstances, they squashed into a small ground-floor flat near the university and Aunt Lena (who married a million-aire and died on a luggage trolley in Glasgow Central Station) looked after them all. Mother told stories of beds in cupboards and wild nights by the kitchen fire, drinking hot water seasoned with pepper and salt.

The boys went to war and the girls became secretaries. Ma, the youngest, went to a cookery college affectionately known in Glasgow as the

Dough School, where she started her career as an inspired cook and learnt to wash walls down before New Year with vinegar in the rinsing water. Then she joined her sisters at the *Glasgow Herald* offices where she met my father.

He must have been a stumbler for a girl. Handsome, gifted and wounded in the First World War, I think he had what we now call post-traumatic stress disorder. I don't know when Ma ripped her mournful wedding pictures out of the family album, but seven-year-olds are perfectly able to recognise unhappiness.

I only met Father properly years later, after he had eloped with his landlady's daughter, but I was eighteen by then and it was too late for love.

I remember 3 September 1939 and the outbreak of war. We were to be evacuated. It sounded painful and some of it was. At school we were just 'the evacuees', 'wee Glasgow keelies', and they snapped the elastic on my hat till my eyes watered. I caught fleas and lost my gas-mask. James, my brother who was twelve, wet the bed, got whacked with a slipper and ran away back to the bombs. I was left behind.

My mother and my brother were now half-term and holiday treats. Thinking about it now, I feel bereft. I missed such a lot of warmth. Mother was good at warmth. She always had a gift for dispelling gloom, a useful talent in 1940s Glasgow, which must have attracted Uncle Arthur who, though witty, had a dark side. He used to cheer himself up with the aunts – their brother John was his best friend – but they were all spoken for, so when Mother was divorced he came courting.

She had taken a job in a ladies' boutique called Penelope's, opposite Craig's tea-rooms and next to the Beresford Hotel on Sauchiehall Street. Here she kept the accounts in a huge ledger in a very neat hand, wearing a very neat suit.

On Saturday, she served everybody in the back shop delicious savoury baps before she locked up. I loved the back shop, where Mother removed Utility labels from clothes and replaced them with others she had acquired. Now and again, if she came by a good piece of meat, she would sear it on a high flame on the single gas ring, wrap it in layers of greaseproof paper, a napkin and brown paper and send it by post to anyone she thought deserving at the time.

Arthur and Ma married when I was thirteen and away at boarding school in Bristol. They were very happy. Mother had discovered that men can be funny. If ever I was in a position to phone home, they were never being bombed. Instead they were playing riotous games of 'Russian' ping-pong.

One bomb did bring down all the ceilings in the close stairwell with such a rumbling crash that Joey the budgerigar flew up the chimney and never came down again.

Whatever was happening, Ma always travelled down to Bristol at half term wearing an embarrassing hat on loan from Penelope's. If there was a patch of blue in the sky large enough to make a cat's pyjamas, she would let out piercing yelps, 'Pip-pip', and sing in the street. She also got me seriously tipsy on scrumpy, which she thought sounded harmless.

She and Uncle Arthur moved from their flat to look after Grannie in Aunt Lena's enormous house, where they grew vegetables and longed for their own plot. Every holiday we went for long drives into the country to find the cottage of their dreams. We never found it. Not till I'd married and had a baby.

My husband and I met at the London Old Vic when we 'walked on' in *Romeo and Juliet*. I was a Montague. He was a Capulet. We didn't speak much. But later we all had a very good time at one of the early Edinburgh Festivals, and joined a company that toured the West Country in a bus that held our sets and costumes; we ended up at the Bristol Old Vic in *A Midsummer Night's Dream*, when we proposed to each other. I was Titania. He was Puck.

We got married on a matinée day. Mother bounced into my bedroom that morning, wearing a hat that looked like a chrysanthemum. 'If you don't want to do this, darling,' she said, 'we'll just have a lovely party. It'll be fine.' I felt that explained her mournful wedding photos. No one had offered her an escape route.

It was May. The sun shone. Uncle Arthur gave me away and Mother blew kisses at the vicar. Then the family party, with assorted aunts, drove to France and we went to give a performance.

I wonder what it was like.

We found a flat in London where you filled the bath with a hosepipe from the kitchen tap. We were happy and in modest employment. My new husband took a job as a 'day man' backstage at Sadler's Wells.

Two years later, we had our daughter Emma. It was April. Just in time for the holidays. We had a phone call from Ma. 'I've taken a house on the Clyde,' she announced, like an Edwardian matron. 'I want the baby to start life in good fresh air.'

The weather was appalling. The sea and the sky merged in battleship grey, chucking water at the windows, and our landlady was an alcoholic, who hid our cheques and had regular visits from the police. We took our tin-can car along the purple ribbon of a road that led to the village of Ardentinny, asking at every BandB if they had room for us. They did, but they were too expensive. Then the wind changed and the weather was sublime. We stopped at the Primrose tea-rooms in the village

for an ice-cream, and I sat on the jetty with the baby, dangling my feet in the loch and nibbling a choc ice.

My husband wandered away down the village street to find the phone box, saying that Mrs Moffat in the tea-rooms had told him there were rooms to let in a cottage close by. I had barely finished my ice when he came thundering back down the road at uncharacteristic speed. 'We've got it,' he said. 'It's five pounds for a fortnight. Go and look. Give me Em.' As I left he called, 'It's not the prettiest cottage. It's the one next door.'

Well – The prettiest cottage was empty.

The prettiest cottage was for sale.

The prettiest cottage was exactly what Uncle Arthur and Ma had been searching for for more than a decade.

We pooled our resources and bought it.

The cottage has had nine lives already. Mother and Uncle Arthur outgrew it and moved to an old manse a short trot along the shore road, where they cultivated their vegetable patch and their soft-fruit cage.

the old manse
mess?

In the eighties it became too much for them. Should they move back to the cottage?

Mother was excited.

Uncle Arthur was depressed.

Moving house didn't help, I suppose. The idea to scale down and live in the cottage had been mooted, applauded and discarded at my every visit, year after year. The morning room became a dump for 'stuff'. Old mattresses, an ancient TV, worn-out bedding and pillows, old saucepans and a toaster, a gramophone, gardening tools, two fishing rods and one galosh.

Mother's confidence was gradually dented by falls on the stairs, with coffee in one hand and a portable wireless in the other. Uncle Arthur just fell down backwards. Then there was the discovery we made, while investigating a damp patch in Ma's bedroom, that the roof void was full of bats. They would squeeze through a chink in the plaster round one kitchen pipe and very slowly move down, paw over paw, till Uncle Arthur caught them in a dishcloth and threw them out. Any remarks about protected species did not go down well.

He was ruthless with mice. He put stuff under the sink that looked like black treacle and the mice got stuck in it, like flies on fly-paper, whereupon he lifted them by the tail and flushed them down the outside loo. And that was another thing: no downstairs loo, except the one outside. Tricky.

Then there was the car and the undoubted skill needed to park it off the road and up the steep drive, then some very dodgy manoeuvres to get down again. And there was the time they were struck by lightning. Both phones blew off the wall, filling the house with acrid smoke, and four neat triangular flaps appeared on the lawn, as if someone had lifted the turf with a sharp blade. Spooky.

That New Year the Rayburn exploded. The kitchen walls and every surface were coated with black oil that took three days to lift, and Uncle Arthur, trying to be helpful, threw himself on to the fire in the sitting room along with a log. Sage discussions took place over arnica and quite a lot of whisky. They would move to the cottage in the spring, they agreed, but by the time I left for London, the kitchen was as good as new and they had changed their minds. There was no question of their ever leaving the old place.

That very week I signed a contract to appear in *La Cage aux Folles* at the London Palladium.

Exciting!

Mother rang that evening.

They had sold the house. It was a bad moment. I don't sob a lot – well, I do now, perhaps, but I didn't then. Too vain. My nose would swell to the size of a light bulb. It still does, but now I don't care.

My agent must have been surprised to hear me on the phone after hours and inarticulate, hiccuping with shock.

'This is not some flibbertigibbet actressy thing,' I managed to yelp. 'This is serious.' She took it as such, tried to get me released and failed. The American producers said I would have to pay for all the printed publicity if I left, but I would be allowed to negotiate a week's holiday to include Easter weekend, which extended it a little. My stand-in was alerted and I bet she was good. No one complained. They didn't miss me at all. That's always a worry.

Mother greeted the news of my foray into musical theatre with real delight. Also, she and Uncle Arthur actually seemed excited about their early move. I hadn't bargained for this burst of energy. They were like teenagers, walloping into the Bulgarian plonk and spending happy hours throwing unwanted belongings into the morning room, then taking them back.

Their lovely garden was now less of a burden and seemed, perversely, to flourish on neglect. The vegetable patch was declared redundant and the soft-fruit cage dismantled. Any leaks in the roof were belittled. It only leaks when it rains and the wind is in the wrong direction, they said. Well, Uncle Arthur said. He didn't want to worry the new owners.

I learnt a great lesson from all this. When you're old, as I am now, you must have a 'project'. It can be quite modest, but you must have one. It creates a future for you. It lifts the spirits.

Mine were lifted, too, by riotous rehearsals. I love dancers. I love their energy, their discipline and their courage. And besides all of that, the chorus in *Cage* were funny.

I had a small part and a huge dressing room, which was, apparently, half of Anna Neagle's when she'd played the Palladium. Just along the corridor there was an even larger dressing room filled with male dancers dressed appealingly in cami-knickers, bras, high heels and a large amount of make-up.

Between shows on Wednesday, they organised competitions for, let's say, the most original contents of a handbag. The Best Hat Award was won, I remember, by a dancer wearing a wide-brimmed bush hat decorated with tampons.

I wondered about our Christmas tree.

On occasion, two dancers in improvised nursing outfits, carrying salad servers, would demand entrance to my boudoir and declare they were there to give me an internal examination.

I spent almost a year laughing, taking French lessons and shopping for furnishing materials in Liberty's department store, directly opposite the stage door.

Of course, there were heart-stopping moments. There was a serious panic when Uncle Arthur said a huge pane of glass in the back kitchen of the cottage had cracked from side to side like the Lady of Shalott's mirror. Jim Thomas, his best mate and neighbour, came round at once to find it was only the fine silver trail of a mountaineering slug.

We had arranged between us a date for certain items of furniture to be moved from manse to cottage in preparation for the final push. In the afternoon Mother rang.

'PHYLLIDA!' she shouted. 'We are being pushed out of the house. They've taken away all the furniture. I got them to bring it back immediately.'

I explained.

She was mortified.

I rang the helpful local remover to apologise. He was very understanding and repeated the procedure. Well, he'd known Mother for years.

I had booked my best mate Mildew for my 'week away', and we flew up, hired a small car, filled it with food, cleaning materials and petrol, and planned our tactics. Tactful tactics.

Mother had plans to make presents of various items lurking among the piles of 'stuff' in the morning room. She was particularly keen to give all the old mattresses to her favourite people. 'Jock and Alistair would love one,' she said. She was

Three Mothers (and a camel)

netting
against
the
midge.

← OXFAM
DUNOON

Mildew

143

adamant. Mildew persuaded her to relinquish the idea because they were stained with blood and pee. That did it.

We borrowed 'the blue van' and made quite a few alarming journeys to the dump. Every time I put my foot on the brake a mattress and assorted

rubbish fell on our heads and the back door flew open. We secured it with a discarded pair of Uncle Arthur's trousers.

A plumber had to be called to the cottage urgently as someone had pushed a Sorbo rubber ball down the loo.

> *There was a young plumber of Lea,*
> *Who was plumbing his girl by the sea.*
> *Said the lady, 'Stop plumbing,*
> *There's somebody coming.'*
> *Said the plumber still plumbing, 'It's me.'*

We did a lot of measuring with an alarming metal tape measure. We ordered shelves, handrails and carpeting for the narrow cottage stairs, and installed

Nril suggested a baseball cap.

a celluloid, eye shade?

'daylight' strip lighting in the kitchen. Frightful, but Mother needed an even light as her glaucoma had raised an ugly eye. Sunlight or spotlights or lamplight blinded and confused her. Mildew got extremely bossy and said Mother needed a white stick to warn people that she was a bit dodgy in the eye department, and she *would* walk down the middle of the road as if it was hers. Thank goodness she wasn't deaf and heard the local bus. We tried to paint her walking stick with white gloss, but it didn't take on the varnish, so Mildew wrapped it round with white Fablon, like a bandaged leg. Not elegant, but serviceable, and Mother was charmed. I think.

Mildew's gift for creative bullying was such a help. We were to get up at six thirty sharp, no breakfast, so we'd get through the lists we'd made at midnight.

The weather, as so often round Easter time, was glorious and sometimes we sat at the cottage against the warm wall of the outside loo, drinking tea, picking dirt out of our fingernails and discussing battle plans.

It was all those books, the china cupboards, the drawers of odd clothing, and the boxes to be marked up. What was to go in the first lot, and what was to be left till last, and would they come in time to mend the heater in the hall, which ought to be on *now*? We hadn't enough labels.

And we should arrange food and the fridge, I thought. Mother boiled a wine cork with the potatoes yesterday. Her poor eyes were a bit like Grannie's were – she couldn't judge distance accurately. Grannie used to wave her little paws about near objects of interest, like cakes, and leave her footprints on the icing, and Ma was now missing her target as she made tentative efforts to help, a little like a polite child playing blind man's buff. Mildew said I must learn to put things back exactly where I found them, however odd the place might seem, and I wasn't to get 'creative with the cutlery'.

Uncle Arthur wasn't loving this bit but he loved Mildew and sometimes put his hand up to stroke her cheek. He never did that to me. He said he'd 'just like to know what's going on'.

———

Poor Uncle Arthur. I think I killed him.

DECLINE AND FALL

Well, I made it. Just. The flight was frightful. Approaching Glasgow, the big Boeing 707 started to bounce about like a ping-pong ball. We thumped to the ground and juddered to a halt in a puddle the length of Loch Long. The pilot apologised. 'It was like handling a light aircraft,' he said. The rain was horizontal and my hired Fiesta kept doing the 'pally glide' as the wind hit her about. Then I got stuck in Gourock behind a parade of Boy Scouts going to the war memorial very slowly, kilts dripping, bagpipes wailing and water-logged.

It was dark when I reached the ferry and the queue was enormous. I rang Mother from the phone box to tell her I might have to stay the night at the hotel along the coast that looked like a set of shelves and I'd catch the early ferry but she'd left the phone off the hook again. She will do that.

arrive tomorrow so I'll pick her up from the ferry and we'll do a major shop at the Co-op. Sophie is in charge of décor: the sitting room is in need of attention as the minister is to give his peroration there after we get back from the 'creamer' in Gourock. Family will go over the water and we'll be back for the village party.

Mrs Waddell is going to stand on her head. She was a PE teacher and will stand on her head anywhere without notice. I can't wait.

———

Dear Em!

It would be good if you phoned around 6 p.m. when I fully intend to be thoroughly inebriated and Ma will have had her G and T. She is remarkable really. Tonight she is cooking a new recipe she found and wishes me to sample and pass comment. I don't like to tell her I have had it every visit for the last couple of years. It is fillet of fish – I think it is cod – and she bakes it spread with tomato ketchup.

I know. Sounds disgusting.

Sophie and I will contribute to the funeral baked meats. Looking up Mother's recipes in the old filing box I found this re game: 'Daudet compared its scented flesh to an old courtesan's flesh marinated in a bidet.'

———•——

She did it. Mrs Waddell.
In the middle of Rev.
John's eulogy she sidled
up to me and whispered,
'Shall I do it now?' and she
did it. She tucked her tweed
skirt between her legs and
up she went. Just like that.
It was a great success.
Such a useful talent. Besides
which she knits toys. I have a spectacular policeman and a
very good Shake-
speare in pink and
green with waggly legs and
a tragic expression.

Rev. John was a
star. He was utterly
unfazed and very
funny about Uncle
Arthur and the price
of soup in Heaven. The
village was there, of course,

155

all the chaps in their black ties, and one nurse from the ward brought her husband in a kilt. Mother was very gracious.

'He had the time of his life in hospital,' she said. I blew my nose. He was vitriolic to the doctor, rude to the old man opposite and insulting to the nurses. A couple of pills for depression, and they all got a handsome apology, or so they say.

Mrs Pennycuick (the one who can't reverse in her car) came with a photo of her new grandchild. Mother peered at it with her monocle, cooed a lot and asked how old the puppy was.

There was a bit of a panic when wee Mrs Wishart asked for a sherry and we had none. Mildew saved the day by mixing Southern Comfort with the dregs of some posh dessert wine she found. Apparently it was delicious.

After a noisy search in the herb department, she found a quarter-bottle of rum behind the Branston Pickle. We must always remember to keep some, as Eric the builder drinks nothing else and he has been so brilliant. He came along immediately when Uncle A pulled the radiator off the wall. The other booze held up very well, which was a blessing as Ma made me promise not to put a kettle on. Too much trouble. 'Open a bottle!' she used to shout at Uncle A. 'Open a bottle.' And there, helpfully, is the handle he hung on to when going into curtsy-sitting to view the 'cellar' (i.e. a box under the stairs).

They used to shout at each other a lot and I think they enjoyed it thoroughly. 'How do you find your mother?' he asked me, last time I was up.

'Not good,' I said. 'She hasn't slept well, she felt sick this morning and she says you're a *shit*.' He fell about.

I always loved his silent fits of giggles. They were the best bit when I was young, for he wasn't cut out to be a stepfather. He distrusted the young and treated them like unexploded bombs, which always indicates, I think, a misspent youth on the part of the critic, tho' it must be frightful to inherit prefabricated children. I was thirteen and away at boarding school when Mother married Uncle Arthur, and affection only blossomed between us when I could cook. And drive a car. I drove him across London once and he never quite recovered.

———•———

Why do funerals make one HUNGRY? I have just wolfed a huge slab of flapjack. Mother went to bed flattened but pleased 'the party' had gone so well, and she isn't wheezing very much at all now. She always used to get bronchitis on any large family occasion. My childish heart got very heavy when I heard her clearing her throat and checking on her breathing. She gave up smoking years ago, but what I didn't know was that saltwater is very bad for people with 'chests' and what is more Ma used to plunge into the loch every day. Dorothy-next-door and her husband both had emphysema and the doctor told them they should move inland and as far from saltwater as they could go. Too late. I can't move Mother again. Anyway, she's safely tucked up now. Last night there was a glorious burst of wheezing hysterics from her room when Soph pinned her down to remove some visible whiskers with my eyebrow tweezers. And then, after a peaceable silence, there were yelps of laughter from Soph, as Mother, hoping for an early bed, said suddenly, 'Time is on the wane as the man said when the clock fell on the baby.' (Wain is Scots for 'baby'.)

How is it that elderly people are so surprisingly cheerful about death? I remember dreading to tell Gran that Aunt Min had died but it seemed to give her a new lease of life. I suppose shock comes into it. Or George Mackay Brown's 'undersong of terrible holy joy'.

Em rang. We are keeping all the details till later. Told her the flowers were fabulous and so they were. Soph found an eccentric amount of tins, jugs and enamel basins to fill the cottage. Em gutted, of course, but Uncle A would have thought it mad to board a plane from America even if she could, and he wouldn't have hung around for anyone. He was fed up last time I saw him in the garden here. He was standing, stick in hand, fastidiously dressed, tie neatly knotted, smelling of Vetiver. 'There's no decency left in the world,' he said, and left for lunch with Jim Thomas.

I know we've done the easy bit. Tomorrow is another day. Who said that? Shakespeare? Scarlett O'Hara? Soph has to leave tomorrow, so I'll drop her at the ferry, have a quick sob, and go into the solicitor's with Uncle A's attaché case. He told me it holds everything and in perfect order. I don't doubt it. He had a degree in financial integrity.

Got to go to bed.

Peerless morning. Typical. Waved Soph off on the ferry, slicing its way through satin smooth water. Did a big shop at Co-op and called on the solicitor. (He's the one who defended a guy who wore a balaclava and stood in the queue to rob the bank on the corner of Argyle Street.) It took relentless bullying by both of us to get Uncle A to sign his will. What is it about men and wills? They think they're going to snuff it while signing, I suppose. Must check Mother's. Where on earth will it be? Perhaps I needn't tell her that I saw Uncle A's latest bank statement. He had precisely £309.56 left in the world. No wonder he worried about the price of soup.

Came home to a quick lunch of leftovers. We dipped all the sandwiches in beaten egg and fried them. Delicious. Still tidying up. Found a copy of J. B. Priestley's *Delight* lying face down in the bothy. It was a bit rumpled but it had fallen open at a passage in which he said the book was a penitence 'for having grumbled so much, for having darkened the breakfast table, almost ruined the lunch, nearly silenced the dinner party – for all the fretting and chafing, grousing and croaking, for the old glum look and the thrust-out lower lip'. Uncle Arthur to a T.

Uncle Arthur had a stutter quite as bad as good King George's. This made chatting rather hard work at first, and I never sat and questioned him in a companionable way. I knew he had followed his father into the egg trade, because he had an obscure relative who marketed eggs on the hoof, as it were, by driving flocks of geese, turkey and hens across Russia, wearing little shammy-leather bootees to protect their feet. He would herd them onto ships, where, safely 'cooped' they laid their eggs for weeks all ready to be sold on arrival. And he had a scary aunt Dodie, who taught English to a posh family in 'Leningrad' and was paid in Fabergé eggs.

She auctioned them for the Free French and they made a fortune, unlike the eatable variety. I don't think there was much money in eggs. During the war, of course, they were nationalised. Uncle Arthur remained attached throughout the duration, and enjoyed his business life. 'He's a man's man,' Mother would say, and 'What did you have for lunch today, dear?' There was always 'lunch with the boys'. Beef olives seemed popular. I'm not sure what they are. Nothing to do with olives.

I met him once, Priestley. He came to the Glasgow Citizens Theatre during rehearsals for one of his plays. Was it *Mr Gillie*? No, that's thing-ummy whatsisname – Bridie. We all had lunch and he seemed really affable. Glorious voice, and the pipe, of course. I nearly ran him over outside Stratford once. He was crossing a country road near his home, Kissing Tree House. You have to love someone who lives in Kissing Tree House.

I've got a part in *Peter's Friends*. Things are taking shape. Life is beginning to look almost manageable. They are fine about missing the read-through. I'm not the only one, but I shall be three days late for rehearsal. Make-up and Wardrobe will ring me here but I'm not on camera till Monday next, which gives me a bit of breathing space. Mildew will have to take me through lines on the plane. It seems most of my stuff will be shot in one week because of the location. Brilliant. I could be back up here in less than two weeks. Then I want to move Ma downstairs to Uncle A's room. Much easier for her and a straight run to the loo. I will get rid of the old sad wardrobe, the bed and that distressing chest of drawers. I'll have to borrow the blue van. The room will need repainting. Magnolia? Boring? Different curtains and decent lampshades. Wish I could start now but that would be *rude*.

Sleepless night. I'd forgotten about the car. Mother can't and shouldn't drive it. There's still a rusting scrape on the offside door. She was driving home one evening and, thinking the lighthouse was an oncoming car, she pulled over and fell into a ditch. I decided to drive it back to London and get rid of my mine. Now, at breakfast, Mildew points out that I'll need the car when I get back here. CURSES.

Passed the Glory Hole on my way into Dunoon and, seeing it was open, wandered in to snoop and enquire about what they think they might take from the pile of stuff we'll need to shift. Anyway, there was Mrs Beggs, the good and glorious.

I think it was the minister's wife who told me about Mrs Beggs (the good and glorious). Apparently, she 'looks after people', and when I timidly sketched out my situation, she understood immediately and offered nights for the week I'll be away. I didn't ask, she offered. That means Mother will have Marvellous Marianne in the morning and Mrs Beggs at night. Result! Beggsie can come to tea tomorrow, but Ma knows her well of old when she used to run a bakery in Dunoon, so that doesn't worry me. What does is that she'll have to sleep in Uncle Arthur's gloomy bedroom. I explained. Fine. I love her.

———•———

It was a wild morning. Window wide, polish akimbo, Marigold gloves and Frish. I took all the linen, curtains and coverlet to the laundry. The coverlet is really nice and at least the curtains will smell fresh. I'm going to throw away the electric blanket. It's got a huge brown singed corner where Ma left it on and it caught fire. Pong was frightful, but nobody died.

That white tray-cloth with the crocheted edges will cover the top of the dismal chest of drawers and then a jug of fresh flowers – no, they won't last. I'll get a pot of something. An African violet perhaps. Mildew says the dingy drugget is a hazard.

Glory Hole? I'll clean the carpet. Bex Bissell is on the shopping list. Feathers keep bursting out of one of the old yellowing pillows. I'll stitch it into a clean pillow case but it should be cleaned. It's disgusting.

Mother, thank heavens, barely noticed the disruption. We gave her coffee sitting in the doorway of the shed, out of the sun, before her morning walk. I shouted at her as she trotted down the path with Marianne, waving her stick, 'You haven't got your distance glasses on, Mother.'

FOUND in mother's knicker drawer.

BR. 25761

BRITISH RAILWAYS
LONDON MIDLAND REGION

SLEEPING CAR SURVEY OF DRUGGETS

This small mat or drugget is for use when changing. For some time we have been experimenting with different types of material and we feel that this specimen disposable drugget made of a new type synthetic fibre may be the most suitable for this purpose.

The disposable synthetic drugget is more hygenic but before making a decision we want to know whether it meets with our customers' approval. I hope you will help us to make the right decision from the passengers' point of view by filling in the brief questionnaire which is given below and handing it to the Sleeping Car attendant.

Thank you for your co-operation.

R. A. TAYLOR,
Passenger Manager

July, 1966

PLEASE WRITE OR TICK (√) ANSWERS IN THE SPACES PROVIDED.

1. Have you had previous experience of using a drugget ?   Yes ☐ No ☐

2. Do you favour the synthetic drugget ?   Yes ☐ No ☐

3. Have you any improvements to suggest to this new type of drugget ?

Good word for Scrabble, 'Drugget'.

Hat on backwards today

'Don't worry, dear,' she said. 'I'm not going any distance.'

Turning our attention to larder and fridge: we'll do a basic shop at some point but I think a visit to the Oyster Bar on Loch Fyne would do us good, whatever the weather. Smoked salmon and a piece of Bradan Rost are on the list and they will keep.

I could make a kedgeree before I go. It will have to be Dunoon for a piece of ham. If I boil and bake it, I can use the stock for lentil soup and put some in the deep freeze. Lentils go off so suddenly and start to bubble volcanically. I suggested a pot of mince but Ma isn't keen. Indigestible, she said. She asked for mushrooms on toast for lunch and I made it, with supervision, as she used to do, with cream and nutmeg.

Must get more cream. I'll get peppers, tomatoes and anchovies for that Delia Smith recipe. And garlic. Uncle A forbade it. Ma used to try and sneak it into everything, tucking it under the leg of lamb

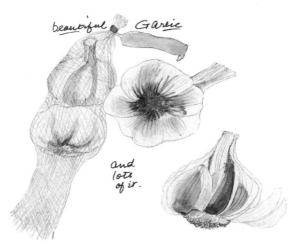

beautiful Garlic

and lots of it.

or near the bone. 'He'll never know,' she'd say. He always did. He hated it so much I gave him a handsomely illustrated book on garlic for Christmas one year. Lovely photos. That was where I got the tip to push a clove up your bum if you had piles. Nor would he eat avocados. He said they tasted of soap. There are some days when I agree. He thought he didn't like Brussels sprouts either but Ma used to put them with soft boiled potatoes and create a sort of beautiful pale green mash, which he loved. If he asked her what it was she'd say, 'A whim-wham for a goose's bridle', which was always her lie about rabbit when we were kids.

I'll buy a couple of packets of Jus-Rol pastry for a 'perhaps pie'. And two dozen eggs as I bet she'll make us a soufflé on our last night. It always makes me sad. A soufflé. She always made one for supper the night before I left for boarding school. Followed by apple crumble. She saved the fat and sugar specially. I'd just have liked baked potatoes and salad. There's tons of cheese. In fact, I'll grate all the dry old bits of this and that and make potted cheese.

DEVILLED CHEESE

½ cup cream
2 cups tasty cheese
1 tsp English made mustard
Dash of Tabasco (bet we have none)
2 tsp Worcestershire sauce

Melt all together over low heat until smooth and creamy. (Ma has written in a firm young hand DON'T BOIL.)

———•———

At breakfast this morning (we had breakfast this morning), and looking to hear the weather forecast, I listened to a very moving account of someone with the fatal disease Huntington's Chorea. It's difficult to diagnose but early symptoms include a funny walk, when you veer off in odd directions, leaving taps running or lit fags everywhere.

That's me. Aside from the fags. When I got up this morning I was definitely veering. Like the weather forecast 'veering south and losing identity'.

Mildew says her elegant friend Iris found herself on a bus, neatly dressed as ever, with a plastic bag of potato peelings on her lap. Trying to appear nonchalant, she put them in a bin and, greatly relieved, tried to open her front door with her Freedom Pass.

However, I did remember to put the milk can out for Jimmie Helm and ran down to see him when I heard all the clanking. He doesn't like this dry spell. 'It's nae guid for dumb animals,' he said. I think he waters the milk: it's a bit blue.

In the back of his van there is this little creature, straight-backed and silent, with solemn, unblinking blue eyes under a hand-knitted bonnet. The only thing about her that isn't knitted is her wellies. I could eat her. She doesn't belong to

Jimmie, she's just there for the ride. A mascot, guarding his milk can.

I asked for news of the glen and the Hatricks. I haven't seen Bertie since the tea-room closed. He used to walk the two or three miles there and back for a few 'penny joys' and some fags. He'd put a penny down, get his toffee and repeat the process till he ran out of pennies. When Em was tiny she would sit at a table with him while he had his cup of tea; they were fascinated by each other. Once she told him she thought he ought to have a bath and he gravely accepted the idea. Don't think he followed it up. His mum and dad were first cousins. I never met them. Dad had been a policeman. A big man, when he died they couldn't get his coffin round the bend in the farmhouse stairs and had to lower him out of a window.

Gossip is sadly thin since the tea-rooms closed. It was a brilliant source.

What has happened to the McDaids? I wonder. Prison? They stole blocks of cooking chocolate from the tea-rooms and cleaned the post office out of Rennies. Then they went and milked Bridget the

cow and fell asleep against her sides with her udder as a pillow. Fearless wee monsters.

For some reason, Mother has started calling Mildew 'Doolie'. Names have never been her bag. She used to call Captain Peacock of *Are You Being Served?* Colonel Sparrow, and renamed the canary 'Wee Wheel' when he'd been known as Diggory from birth. We thought he was a chap until he laid an egg, which might have confused the issue, but 'Wee Wheel'? She used to let he/she/it fly

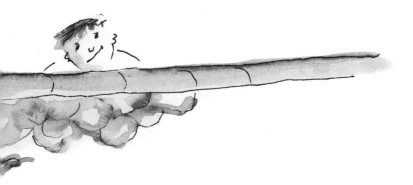

around the kitchen till it ate most of her rubber plant and died. Never let a bird free in a kitchen. Cousin Eleanor's budgie flew into a fan and came out bald.

I wonder if we should get Ma a pet. It's supposed to be good for the old and infirm. I don't think she could cope with a dog. A cat? Mildew says the dog next door would eat a cat. A canary that sings? Wee Wheel didn't, which was a disappointment, but he made up for it by looking like Frankie Howerd

'wee wheek'

owing to a circle of feathers on his head that resembled a tiny toupee.

Wish I didn't have to go home quite yet. I've got that awful it's-Sunday-and-it's-school-tomorrow feeling. Like Ma's soufflé. Sunk in the middle.

Home. Dumped my bag through the door and trotted round the corner for milk, etc. The garden has made vigorous efforts to get into the kitchen.

Rang the cottage. It was engaged for so long I assumed Ma had left the phone off the hook but apparently not. She'd had a long phone call from Jessie commiserating about Uncle Arthur. I think I may have forgotten to ring Jessie with the sad news, which reminds me: I've got a packet of letters to respond to. I'll get Ma some nice cards to send. Good idea. She just needs to sign them.

Costume fitting today. Makeup and hair sorted. I'll do.

Phoned Ma just after six and asked to speak to Beggsie.

'She went home ages ago, darling.' Felt sick. I haven't got Beggsie's number. Had to ring doctor to get it. Apparently Ma cooked tea, they watched a bit of telly and she was sent home. Beggsie says she's working on it. Oh, cripes.

———·—·———

Five a.m. alarm call. Filming tomorrow; pick-up at six fifteen. Laid out all the needful at the front door before I went to bed. Everybody there for dinner scene. Good fun. Wrapped at seven p.m. Home by eight thirty. Rang cottage. No answer. Phone off hook?

Rang Beggsie. No answer.

Rang Marianne. No answer.

This is awful.

Will ring from production office tomorrow. Pick-up six thirty a.m.

———·—·———

Got Ma at breakfast time. She and Beggsie had a lovely evening apparently and it was dark so she had insisted Beggs stay the night.

I suggested (timidly) that perhaps it would be nice if Beggs spent every night with her while I am away and she said I was a 'hulking bully' and could I ring around six p.m.: there is something they want to watch after that. She cooked that fish dish again and is keeping all the scraps for Marianne's new kittens. Marianne is now having a caravan in the back garden exclusively for cats with no birth control. I wonder yet again if a kitten wouldn't be a good idea for Ma.

Hope to goodness I can get near a phone at six p.m.-ish. I can't remember who defined an English-man as someone with insect legs and a pot belly who insists on ringing his mother after six p.m.

Had a great day with no lines to speak of, just looking as if I can cook. Stephen Fry and I skinned and chopped tomatoes. How unlikely is that? Nice scene. Amazing how the young lift lines off a script. Long conversation with Ma on phone about a robin that has adopted the back porch as a surveillance post. It sings. She's thrilled. Maybe a tame robin is enough?

Sunday lunch scene tomorrow.

———————

It was touch and go but I had to concentrate so hard on the order of the cooking pots I hadn't time to worry about anything else. Props chap was astonishing in his grasp of what was needed and when, not to mention steam control. I've still got a slightly pink weal on my left arm and a steam burn on the back of my right index finger.

Both Em and I were picked up this morning at six twenty.

Nice to catch up in the car.

Nice, too, to work with Em around.

I seem to belong more when she's there. Won't stop for the wrap party. I'd be like a cabbage in a petunia patch. And anyway I must whiz back to let Beggsie get home to her own bed. Still, it's been a 'Nice Job', as Jack Nicholson said after *Five Easy Pieces*.

Great timing. It's one hour thirty minutes to Heathrow on the Tube. Standby flight almost as soon as I hit BA lounge. Hired car. Caught ferry. Home by teatime. Five hours door to door this time.

———•—

Everyone always asks what it's like to work with my daughters. There's clearly a suspicion that it could be tricky. In fact, it's incredibly nice. For me anyway. For a start we occupy different strands of the profession and are unlikely to audition for the same part.

Just on a practical level, we know we don't take sugar in tea or coffee and one or other of us will know where the loo is. We are used to sharing small spaces, cleansers, cotton wool and make-up, though I draw the line at toothbrushes. We know about nerves, when to talk, when to shut up and who will be carrying which medical supplies. It's a fantastic and reassuring support system, which includes that most treasured ingredient; trust.

In a film called *The Winter Guest*, Emma and I played mother and daughter. No research required. You're ahead of the game. And I was sort of pulled along. We would pile into a unit car at some ungodly hour and Em would say, 'Right Ma. From the top.' Every day. Fierce.

Playing Sophie's mother in the film *Emma*: bliss. I barely said a word. She had them. Companionable travel again.

———————

Caught Mother doing a 'boarding-school strip' this morning, or what she calls 'washing her forks'. I nearly fainted. There was a long dark gash on her stomach as if she had been shot or her appendix scar had exploded.

It turned out she'd put a felt pen in her trouser pocket and it had leaked through three layers. I'll never get the ink out of her breeks. They're in soak 'for the now'.

I realise I should have listened to Mildew. A shower would be the very thing. I think the moment has arrived. The bathroom could do with some attention anyway and we need a project. Rang Eric. He'll take the bath. Dunoon tomorrow. We'll have a look at tiling and Mother can drop into Sandra Graham to look for shower curtains and other such. I'll never get her out of there.

Suggest to her that we stay overnight in Glasgow at the RAC Club in Blythswood Square when Eric fits the shower. This goes down rather well.

Very successful trip 'to town'. Mother did extremely well. We were both dreading it as she would be bound to meet folk who would offer their condolences on Uncle Arthur's sad departure. It had to be done and we did it.

At one point I left her chatting away with the McWhirters and dashed into Purdie's to buy a pair of socks for my wellies. I couldn't find her when I came out. She had climbed into the passenger seat of a strange car to the mild astonishment of the elderly driver. Stayed for ages chatting to him and Brian, the parking person, who was about to book the driver and didn't. Smiles all round. We went and bought a shower cap in Marshall's.

On the way home there's a faded old advert painted on the brick gable of a dry cleaner's acclaiming 'VIROL' in faded pink.

'"Anaemic girls need it,"' we cried in unison.

'"Zeebo for grates,"' sang Mother.

'"Ovaltine for night starvation,"' we shouted, and what about Pond's Cold Cream?

'Darling, you look tired,' says the handsome husband, a euphemism for 'You look perfectly frightful and I've every right to leave you tonight.'

Maybe that's the reason I always had Pond's Cold Cream to take my make-up off when I was in rep.

I used to buy a whopping great jar, which once fell off a shelf in my digs and crashed straight through the china wash basin. It cost eight pounds to replace. I was being paid five pounds per week.

Mother came out suddenly with '"Sausages is the Boys"'! Apparently this was an advert for Wall's sausages on Glasgow trams. Or so she said.

Then she chanted a wee ditty that went something like 'Soon as it crawls, feed your baby with Wall's.' When she worked at a clinic before the war,

a wee woman brought in a very poorly baby who had been weaned on Wall's sausages. The power of advertising. Scary. Ma said men used to shout at the helpers in the clinic, 'Awa' hame and iron yer man's shirt.' I believe she gave lectures on cooking and during rationing venison was a real treat, but in some cuts a dry meat.

'It's awful nice if you bury it in the garden for a week or put a wee bit redcurrant jelly to the gravy,' said a voice from the back of the hall.

———————

Driving up to Glasgow for our 'away day', we had only got to Paisley when Mother said reproachfully, 'It's an awfully long way, Phyllida.' This from the woman who wanted to visit her old boyfriend Jack Chown, who lived in Australia.

'It's something like a thirty-six-hour flight to Sydney,' I said.

'Who's he?' she said.

Our visit to the Club was a triumph. Mother was so delighted with everything I felt guilty about not doing it before. It had never occurred to me.

Dinner in the Club dining room was memorable. Almost the best bit. The waiter was enchanted by her. I do think her monocle helps. He paid perfect attention to everything, including her eccentric and habitual request for some caster sugar for the tomatoes in her side salad. Gravely bowing, he gravely returned with a silver sugar shaker. I can't remember now what I ate but Ma had something recommended by her new friend, which I think was called 'Cod dugléré' though it sounds unlikely and looked remarkably like her signature dish of cod in tomato ketchup. Surely not. I think it was in a red wine sauce. Anyway, she pronounced it delicious and the wine chosen by her adviser was also pronounced perfect. She actually managed a crème brûlée. 'This is bliss, Phyllida,' she said. When I stopped to talk to Reception on our way upstairs, I lost her for a beat, only to find her by the lift having an animated conversation with herself in a long mirror. 'There's another plump wee lady with a white stick staying at this hotel,' she said.

Bedtime was revealing. She was like me with a roadmap. I never know which way up it is and I have to get out of the car and stand on it. Then there's Emma, who used never to be able to comprehend that a road goes in two directions. Whichever way I walked Ma through it, she simply couldn't find the bathroom door. I had images of her wandering the corridor in her nightie or shutting herself in the wardrobe, so I left the light on in the loo with the door open.

The cottage is so perfectly familiar to her now that she never has a problem. So there I was, flood-lit and wide awake, when Ma got up to pee and she still got lost. I think the light was a mistake. Too bright. It does seem to blind her and why, after all, should she know where the hell she is in the middle of the night and a strange place?

Mildew is coming up for a few days. There's to be a formal opening of the new bedroom and the shower. I need to reinstall the cork tiles and haven't got the right glue. Curses. Then one fine day we will fork Uncle A's ashes round his roses, as requested.

Went into the Bothy to check the bed linen. The night-store heaters are on already and the bunker is full of coal but the cludgie is a bit damp. I'll check the rhone pipe tomorrow. The drainpipes are probably blocked but the flush is reassuringly violent.

Walked into the wee parlour and found the rag rug glittering with shattered glass. Uncle Arthur's ashes were sitting innocently on the mantel but somehow my picture of Buxton the crow had fallen and smashed on the hearth.

Did he fall or was he pushed? I recovered the ashes from the mantel, placed them in the dresser cupboard and snibbed the door carefully.

I love Buxton. He's painted in bitumen by a nice young man along the coast. Uncle A thought him perfectly frightful and wouldn't give him house room.

———•———

Three Mothers (and a camel)

Dear Mildew,

The Bothy is ready and waiting. A Bothy (since you ask) is a basic shelter, usually left unlocked and available for anyone to use free of charge! This is the deluxe version with a large bottle of last year's damson vodka sitting on the dresser beside a dainty crystal glass. Actually it is a tumbler. Your bedroom looks inviting and I have the electric blanket on already. Personally, I miss the sound of Bridget the cow kicking the walls, but you would just let her out to roam on the main road and bump into buses.

She's gone off to the farm. It's all right, she won't be burgers, she is a milker. I know a lot about cows. I played one in panto known as 'the udder half'. The front half was my erstwhile mate Lisa, who was half Italian and had to be forbidden beans and garlic. Which reminds me, Uncle Arthur's ashes are in the dresser cupboard. Don't sprinkle them on your cocoa. They were on the mantelpiece. I feel convinced that Uncle A pushed Buxton the crow off

*his perch and broke the glass. Quite a good thing
in the end as I had to clean the rag rug and sweep
the lino.*

*I envy you moving in there. The weather is vile
and an equinoctial gale is blowing (don't ask) and
the thing about the Bothy is its soothing atmosphere.
I think it's because it is tucked into the corner by
Mr Richardson's farm so the wind and the rain
ignore it and rush off to irritate cottages with a
view of the loch. I haven't slept on my futon in the
Bothy all this trip. There's still a bucket under
the skylight.*

*So much to discuss. Bring your measuring tape.
Let me know which ferry you might catch. It'll be
around five p.m.-ish and I'll pick you up. It's time
to leave Mego for a couple of hours. I think. We can
belt into the Co-op for stores. Yippee. Drear.*

*PS (1) Mego wanted to roast you belly of pork for a
treat. She has quite ignored the fact that you are a
raving vegetarian.*

PS (2) Do you think Mego should have a dog?
Discuss.

PS (3) What do you know about the drug Diamox?
Mego calls it Dime-a-box.

———·—·———

Tonight we discussed dogs. Should Mego have one? Research into all the possibilities ended with Mego in wheezing hysterics as Mildew detailed the dogs of her time.

There was Bitos, the Afghan hound, who bit people on the nose if they smelt of alcohol.

Finn McCool, the Irish wolfhound, had epilepsy and frequently destroyed furniture while having fits and falling downstairs. He was so tall he could look through the letterbox at the sound of a bell and his great golden eyes glaring at the intruder were quite enough to deter entry.

Then came Mick the Greek, a stray mongrel. He became devoted to Mildew's alcoholic monkey, Chico, who was allowed to ride him side-saddle as he patrolled the house, when he would wave graciously to his audience and pat the other dogs as he passed.

Then came Eric, the Welsh terrier, who went bald at an early age and died after an altercation with a lorry in Hampstead Road. After a decent interval Arthur took over. Named after Uncle Arthur, of course. Normally a fearless beast, he hides in the washing machine on Firework Night.

I've got a photo somewhere.

All monkeys are alcoholic, apparently, and Chico was no exception. Mildew used to take him to the pub. Port-and-brandy was his favourite. Mother approved – it's one of hers. I wondered why Bitos didn't bite Chico if he smelt of alcohol, but at any sign of dissension Mildew would put him in his cage in the bathroom where he threw poo at people. Bitos the Afghan just hated men in uniform and used to fling himself at them like an enormous flying duster.

Mother would like a monkey now.

It was a successful supper. The nut loaf was declared delicious and there's plenty to cut cold tomorrow, but it was the carrots that were the sensation of the evening. I used Aunt May's hefty old frying-pan and cooked them very slowly in masses of butter till they were really soft and then added a hefty slug of the sweet sherry Mildew had brought for the store cupboard in case wee Mrs Wishart should call again. We've also got half a bottle of manzanilla sherry in the fridge for our next fish supper.

———•—

The weather was kind and, thank heavens, quite calm, so Mildew and I decided that today was the day.

We gave Ma a gin and tonic, equipped ourselves with two glasses of wine, a garden fork and a hoe. I took the left-hand border, Mildew the right, and we carefully allowed an ounce or two of Uncle Arthur around each of his beloved roses. Every time we had forked some neatly in, we raised a glass, ending up at the gate in good order and ready for a refill. No one walked by on the road. Our only audience was two seagulls sniggering and a school of eider ducks passing their usual comment, like ladies reading *Hello!* magazine. And Mother, of course, at the sitting-room window.

'You have been busy, girls,' she said. 'Were you clearing up the beach?'

It's distance she can't judge. She just saw us moving back and forth on her horizon.

I haven't told her about the ashes. I couldn't. I'll wait till she asks. Maybe she won't.

———·——

Pottering about the kitchen this evening, washing up after supper, polishing the glasses and arranging them in the dresser cupboard, removing some dead leaves from the jug of flowers, straightening the pictures, writing a shopping list and scrubbing the kitchen table, I thought how lucky women are, really. There's always something to DO.

What is a soothing useful occupation for a chap when the weather is bad? Tying feathers on a fish hook? They don't like a walk except with a dog. Uncle Arthur managed a short effort if there was an end in sight, such as soup. He liked his car but

somebody elses
← jumper

← mildew
marigolds

← niqué
(mine)

← sophies
jeans

that had been a grave source of anxiety in recent years. Sophie went with him into Dunoon last time she came up and says it shortened her life. He kept forgetting to use the clutch to change gear.

In this domestic mode of mine, I am going to paint Ma's bedside-cabinet thing a Milly-Molly-Mandy green. The paper lantern lights are up and look lovely. Curtains a triumph. Not too Laura Ashley. We plan a grand opening. I am going to put a ribbon across the door for Ma to cut at 'cocktails'. We might sing a bit. Mildew came into the kitchen this evening and asked, 'What's Praddles, Drear? Mego says it must be time for Praddles.'

It's the cocktail hour apparently.

Ma and the aunts went to France for a holiday and always had what they called Praddles at eleven in the morning and it now conveys cocktails at any hour of the day. I think there must have been a beach bar called Praddles.

Pradels? *Près d'elles?* (Perhaps it's a corruption of pre-prandials.)

Anyway, the name stuck.

I do see that straightening pictures and polishing the taps could simply be a diversionary tactic. I think I'd rather clean the oven than deal with the letters and cards of sympathy still in my case. What I'll do now, I think, is release Mildew from sentry duty and read Mego a bit of *Little Dorrit*. Beggsie has got to Chapter Twelve. Mildew wondered if we should get one of those tape-recording machines provided by the RNIB. Mother says that's nonsense. She is only 'slightly blind'.

'I'm blind to about here,' she said to Mildew, indicating waist level.

Left Mildew in riotous charge and shot into Dunoon to do boring bits. Drew a hundred pounds – a third of Uncle A's estate – and tucked it into an old brown envelope on which I'd written my shopping list. Heading off to the high street, I was sidetracked by Mrs Delmahoy and stopped to have a coffee at the Tudor Tea-rooms. When I finally reached the chemist the envelope was gone. Rushed round all the shops to check – Bell's the draper, Black the baker, Kent the butcher. No sign. Pelted in a panic to where I'd parked the car on the front and there was the envelope in the middle of the main road being run over by a tourist bus. I'd taken off my raincoat and plonked it on top of the car while rootling in the passenger seat for my carrier-bags. Envelope had slipped into the road. Uncle Arthur would have gone purple and into curtsy-sitting.

Money was still there, though.

Sleeping deeply when Sophie rang from Bristol at eleven thirty p.m. Spoke till twelve fifteen a.m. Ma woke at five thirty for some reason. The strange room, perhaps? Feel stewed.

Washing up this evening, Mildew suddenly said, 'My mother wanted me to marry a saucepan salesman.'

She's off tomorrow.

Surprisingly good day today, although I appear to have put a nail through the telephone system. Lovely.

Planted wallflower seedlings at the cludgie door and cleared the Bothy 'garden' a bit. Mildew left all in good order and I can smell polish and bleach.

Redid flowers in the cottage and had two very successful walks with Ma.

Threw thirty-six snails onto the beach.

———•••———

Cooked 'Tomatoes Whittington' for tea.

Cut tomatoes into halves. Heat 3 oz butter or more in a frying pan. Put tomatoes in the foaming butter, cut side down. Puncture the rounded side with a sharp knife. Cook for five minutes. Turn over and cook for ten minutes. Turn again (Whittington); the juices from the tomatoes will have spread around the pan. Turn again – cut side up now. Pour a good slug of cream around them – about three tablespoons. Cook till it bubbles. Serve immediately and eat with warm bread.

Buttered. Didn't care. It went down well.

———•••———

This morning Mother said, in magisterial tones, 'Superior persons never make long visits.'

Mrs Wishart had come to tea and stayed till ten p.m.

———•———

'I make it my business to be happy. Life is bloody awful enough without being unhappy.' Alice Thomas Ellis

———•———

Mother's glaucoma has raised an ugly eye again. Fortunately it's the blind one, or the nearly blind one. And fortunately we had an appointment this very week with Dr Esakowitz who said a small operation would be advisable as she might otherwise lose the eye. Mother was thrilled about the operation. I admire her enthusiasm. I'd do anything to avoid an operation but the thought of Ma in a black eye-patch is rather appealing. Besides which she has blind faith (unfortunate phrase) in Mr Escalope, as she calls him. They get on famously and she is actually looking forward to a stay in Paisley. Well, there is no doubt her eyesight is decidedly worse. The other night, dozing by the TV, she opened her eyes and said, 'Is that you, dear?' to a black singer playing the piano.

Before Mildew left she painted the edges of the step at the front porch with white gloss as Ma simply launches herself into space.

Took great satisfaction today in throwing out Uncle Arthur's soap cage. Every time a tablet of soap was too small, wrinkled and ravaged to use, he would put it into this wirework cage thing, like prison for a tennis ball. Multi-coloured remnants of soap were squidged together into a horrid lump. The cage thing was then hung in the toothbrush department and we were to use it by swooshing it around in the bath or the washbasin causing a feeble approximation of soap suds. Grannie Annie used to do the same. It'll be a war thing. Now we've got a shower and 'soap on a rope', which is worse.

Also, I've burnt another pan. I don't under-stand electric stoves. Can't get this one to simmer.

I suppose I should just have soaked the lentils but I put them on to boil to save time and I was cleaning the leeks when there was a loud 'Yoo-hoo' from the sitting room. Ma had spotted Dorothy-next-door coming up the path with yesterday's post. She wouldn't stop for coffee but the pair of us stood in the porch yakking and then wandered down to the gate together and yakked some more. Then Jimmie Helm came with the milk and he joined in. By the time I got back to the kitchen it was full of smoke and the pan with its lentils was past saving. I took the battery out of the smoke alarm ages ago. The noise was, as Mego put it, 'unacceptable'.

I've soaked the saucepan to no immediate avail. Mildew says dishwasher tablets will do it. We haven't got a dishwashing machine. The tablets are on the shopping list, with lentils.

VENISON STEW

2½ lbs diced venison
2 oz butter
2 tbsp oil
3 onions
2 or 3 cloves of garlic
1 rounded tbsp plain flour
1½ pints good stock
¼ pint red wine
15 oz pickled walnuts

Brown meat first. Keep warm. Soften onions, add garlic, then flour, and make sauce with stock and wine. Put meat back and add walnuts. Put it into the oven at gas mark 4 for 1½–2 hours. Ma has written at the end, 'I have now and then added prunes.'

Must remember redcurrant jelly. I've put the stew in the deep freeze as a treat for our return from Paisley. Nearly went mad trying to find tops for Ma's Tupperware. Jim Thomas says you can't miss the hospital. D'you want to bet?

Ma excited and very pleased with her new dressing-gown.

According to Ma, the surgeon patted her hand and told her she had done very well. She says she was behind a green screen and heard only a scraping noise. Ouch.

When I came to take her home she was a little delayed by a final check on the eye, and as I was packing her bag, she came in on the arm of her lovely Mr Escalope, looking very pink and pretty and enviably elegant in her new tartan dressing-gown, as if she were about to move into a bit of ballroom dancing. She then caused a lot of mirth in the ward of six ladies as she wandered off looking for the loo.

'She's been here three days and she still can't find it,' they whispered. 'It's over here, dearie'; 'Over here, pet'; 'No, no, darling, turn round the other way.'

We finally got it together, collected her pills and her drops, and I even found the car keys. Then there was the problem of finding the car. I never take time enough in a car park to visualise exactly where I put it. Lovely to get in at last. Like getting home. And there were Maynards wine gums in the glove compartment.

Ma sat chatting and chewing when round about Fort Matilda she suddenly said:

'I take three blues at half past eight
To slow my exhalation rate
Alternate nights at nine p.m.
I swallow pinkies – four of them.
The reds, which make my eyebrows strong,
I eat like popcorn all day long.
The speckled browns are what I keep
Beside my bed to help me sleep.
The long flat one is what I take
If I should die before I wake.'

How in Heaven's name did she remember all that and from where? I'd never heard it before in my life. She would suddenly come out with a quote from Shakespeare, quite often very apt, and she knew all the lyrics from 'Miss Otis Regrets'.

And then, when she got home, she went upstairs to her old bedroom. She hadn't quite grasped the concept of downstairs yet.

Might have been the effect of a good glass of Bulgarian and a most delicious stew.

———•—

Sally-next-door broke her key in the lock of her front door and could get neither out nor in. Well, obviously not out. She was in. But if she'd been out she couldn't have got in. D'you see?

Anyway, she pushed one of the kids out of the window and he came for help. We rang John. He came and replaced the lock at vast cost. We had lunch.

At teatime, another child arrived at the door asking for the doctor's number. Oscar had pushed Finbar over and he had cut his finger badly. They pelted off to A and E and our supper was late. Mego filleted. She tried to go upstairs to bed again, still disorientated from the operation. No discernible difference in the eye, but we see Escalope next week. I expect the drugs are making her loopy. A bit loopy.

Just turned down *Tartuffe* director Peter Hall. Well, I can't, can I? Fancy him asking.

Eli rang. She'd been shopping and when she went to pay for her purchases, a frog jumped out of her handbag. It emptied Oxfam. Well, it leaped about like anything, of course.

Frightful screaming in the streets of Sevenoaks.

Cooked three cauli-cheeses and took Mego and Dorothy-next-door to *Robin Hood: Prince of Thieves*. They are none the worse and Mego wheezed with mirth at pretty well all of it. The cinema was particularly quiet when she said very loudly, 'There's Harold'! and as the actor H. Innocent burst upon the screen she started to wave.

So much for her eyesight.

He is quite big on the screen, of course. He is quite big full stop.

————

Going to Glasgow next week. I've got a part in *Taggart*. (There's been a murder – ME.) Marianne will be in most mornings, Beggsie most nights. Emma is coming up for a few days – I'm covered. I'll be 'home' for the weekend. Wonderful. I've always longed to live and work 'at home' so it's thrilling. Rather nervous. They would like my character to be Aberdonian. No chance. I suggested Dunoon. It will be humiliating if my accent is rubbish.

I had nearly finished making Ma's bed this morning, putting top sheet to bottom as per usual, and I was shaking out a clean sheet for the top when I remembered that Charles Laughton's wife Elsa Lanchester said, 'The British never sleep in clean sheets.' I undid the bed, fetched another sheet and started again.

———

I love Glasgow. I love it. I've spent ten days now living and working a sigh away from where I was born in the middle of Great Western Road.

There was the boating pond at Anniesland (I always wondered who she was), the Botanic Gardens, Byres Road, the BBC, the Kelvin river, the bowling green and the steep terrace where we used to hide in a privet hedge, lower a glove on a string so that we could snatch it away when someone kindly bent to pick it up. My brother had a gang. The operational headquarters were in the washhouse in the back green. I was a sort of mascot and allowed to sit on the 'bogey' made out of a floorboard and a set of pram wheels. I did a lot of chores, like spying, and was rewarded sometimes with a toffee apple. That shop has gone; I went to look.

One evening I walked as far as our old tenement and climbed up the stone stairwell to our dark front door. The dank smell of the close was so familiar I very nearly rang the bell, but it was getting dark, I had an early call and I was 'feart'. Our dark doorway was where I remember my mother holding the door open for two men carrying my brother, unconscious after a fall from the washhouse wall. A little trickle of dark blood had hardened on his cheek. I rode my tricycle up and down outside his bedroom just to keep an eye on things.

He didn't die then. He died much later from a serious head injury, as if the first fall had been a warning. A rehearsal. I had to ring my mother from London to tell her James was dying. Hearing my voice on the phone at an unexpected time in the morning, she shouted my name so joyously that I couldn't speak. My teenage daughters sat quietly at the kitchen table, looking down at their laps. Figures of stone.

When they were small they would trace the scar that ran the length of his hairline with their gentle, pudgy fingers.

He had been nearly twenty-four years old when in darkest Buckinghamshire his little convertible, known as 'the pram', slammed into the back of a stationary lorry and he was flung into a field some distance away with assorted injuries that, said the surgeon who replaced most of his head, would significantly shorten his life. How easy it was to bury that information when hope was so high in our hearts, and he used it to build another life, like Ralph in *The Portrait of a Lady*. 'The personality so resulting was delightful; he had to consent to being deplorably ill, yet had somehow escaped being formally sick.'

Instead of being a high-powered hotel manager, he bought the tea-rooms in the village, lit fires, baked and got into the *Good Food Guide*. It was a golden era for us as we crammed into the cottage each holiday and became temporary kitchen staff, eating cakes and sweets and serving them, making pancakes, pouring tea and coaxing cows from out behind the counter. It was arguably harder work than hotel management, and a decade or so later, frail and subject to bouts of debilitating pain known as 'trigeminal neuralgia', he came to live with us in London.

I may have been brought up by James, but my daughters were all his ambition. He was their finishing school. He took them to America, Florence and France, and went to the theatre only if they would accompany him. They watched his courage with careful courtesy and when, in the end, he was on a life-support machine, they stayed with him in Intensive Care, telling stories, singing and reminiscing till everything was switched off at last.

I came each night from the theatre, still smothered in make-up and alarming the nurses. I talked rubbish to him. 'Do you remember how, when I was little and I grazed my knees, you would wipe my snot and tears up with your dirty hanky, promise me bandages and a place in your gang?

'And then how you taught me to tie opposing doorknobs together so that the neighbours couldn't get out?'

I was in the theatre when they switched you off.

The girls were there.

That's enough now.

———··———

The doorway directly opposite ours belonged to the Millers, whose daughter was training to be a doctor. My ambition once. Upstairs lived Mary Ure, who scented the stairwell when she passed by. She became an actress and married the playwright John Osborne.

Mother and Uncle Arthur moved from there after the war to a flat where you were woken at five a.m. by the first tram charging up Great Western Road. I miss the trams. When I worked at the Glasgow Citizens Theatre, I loved going to work by tram and coming home on a noisy Saturday night with my pay in a wee brown envelope, which I gave to Ma. There I was, up from England with my posh voice but awa' home to my mother every night on the tram. The leading actors, Andy Keir and Fulton Mackay, escorted me to my tram stop every night for a week to show the local lads that I belonged and was not to be duffed up. It was the Gorbals, you see.

I missed out on the theatrical digs in Glasgow, which was a pity. I don't know if 'theatrical digs' exist any more. Nowadays we stay in 'hotels', in square rooms where the windows don't open.

Who could forget Mrs Thomas in Exmouth and her thunderbox loo? She looked after half a dozen of us. We travelled all round the West Country in a converted bus, with the sets and costumes in the back, and we played town halls, libraries, schools and Dartmoor Prison. The chaps offloaded the scenery and set it up and the girls ironed and put out costumes, besides being nifty with nails and a hammer. Driving home, sometimes very late from, say, Plymouth or Dorchester, we would discuss food. We always arrived home to a perfect fire roaring in the grate. Mrs Thomas must have heard the bus and whipped in to build it to a peak, before she

slipped away and we tumbled through the door to
a sideboard groaning with comfort food. She did it
on Sundays too.

Then there was Mrs Mackay of Daisy Avenue,
Manchester, who had favourites. She had two
semi-detached houses. Boys in one, girls in the
other and don't flush the WC after ten thirty p.m.

I forget the name of my favourite landlady. As
soon as I arrived she made sure I knew where the
loo was.

'Do you feel the cold, Miss Law?' she asked. 'Because Henry Kendall peed in the basin *here* and took the chromium off the nice new taps.'

We always came home for supper rather smartly after the show. She was a stunning cook and raconteur. She had worked in a munitions factory during the war where the girls became adept at stealing sugar, much used in explosives, I believe, by stitching bags of it into their bras or round the hems of their skirts. Everything got nicked, including scrubbing brushes, which they hung from their suspender belts with tape to get past Security at the gate. 'Oh, when we got to the station, Miss Law, we were red raw down there.'

One girl helped herself to a large wall clock by strapping it round her with roller towels to look as if she was pregnant. 'She'd have got away with it if it hadn't struck the hour.'

Sophie was a pretty good tea-leaf as a student. She walked out of Habitat with two rugs and a chair. She also admits to jars of instant coffee and multivitamins. Em just stole sweeties and got caught.

What concerns me is that Em thinks Ma actually sees things quite well but her brain doesn't always make sense of what they are. A bit like me driving at dusk. Can that be a bear sitting on the hard shoulder? No, it's just a bush and its shadow.

I think that's normal. I hope it's normal.

'How easy is a bush supposed a bear' – *A Midsummer Night's Dream*. Him again.

———•———

Em's gone.

Apparently she helped Mego sort out her wardrobe yesterday.

'Look, darling, you're to have this. It's the very thing for LA. Pure silk!'

She was waving a shiny grey shirt with a postcard-sized label announcing it was 100 per cent nylon.

'And what do you think of my little tank top?' She'd only hacked the sleeves off one of her jumpers. I'll find them, wash and unravel them a bit to blanket stitch the arm holes. Might look quite nice.

Someone said *Jurassic Park* was to be on some TV channel tonight. Probably too late. In any case, Ma said it was just great big animals being horrid to humans.

Took the dictionary to bed. Looked up 'dementia'. It said: 'Any form of insanity characterised by the failure or loss of mental powers; the organic deterioration of intelligence, memory or orientation.'

Calling it insanity is a bit steep surely. Looked up Alzheimer's in Chambers *20th Century Dictionary*, which said, 'Christmas 1959' in my handwriting on the flyleaf.

Alzheimer's wasn't there.

———•———

Was there a Mr Alzheimer?

Yes, there certainly was, a Dr Alois Alzheimer. A portly gentleman, who wore a monocle and chain-smoked cigars, he looked not unlike C. G. Jung.

He worked alongside a distinguished colleague who, it is said, would have liked *his* name to be used, in which case we would all have been afraid of catching Kraepelin. That was his name: Emil Kraepelin. Would you want to give your name to an upsetting condition? He didn't cure it. He just helped to discover it.

Would one want to be Dr Mumps?

Is Alzheimer's hereditary? If so, when does it strike? I think it may have called in already. I lost the car keys this morning. Again. Thank heaven I wasn't meeting anyone off the ferry or something – scoured the house. I even looked in the fridge. Ma once put a new packet of tights in the fridge. She put the bacon in her sock drawer. Such adventures were frequent and not unexpected. She left her wet shoes in the bottom oven of the Rayburn and forgot them. They turned into little stone bootees and Uncle Arthur planted them up with geraniums. Nobody mentioned Alzheimer's. Nobody had heard of it. For me, on days like today, it's a very large elephant in the room. Well, maybe not an elephant for they never forget, do they?

———•—•———

Dr Alzheimer's 'Eureka' patient was a sad lady called Auguste who, in describing her illness to him, said touchingly, 'I have lost myself.'

Mother was lost.

When poor Auguste died there was, of course, a post-mortem. Her brain, that most complex of organs, looked like a clump of unravelled knitting and it had lost the weight of a large grapefruit, besides being disfigured by what are appropriately called 'tangles' and 'plaques', which sound like trouble in the dental department.

'Tangles and Plaques' – a firm of solicitors?

The word 'Alzheimer's' flashes up on a screen in my brain as I wreck the parlour in a geriatric panic. I really need to calm down and walk round slowly with a Geiger counter which would squawk when it found something metallic.

Did I have them in my hand when I pulled those weeds off the wall by the gate? By now, it's raining, of course, so I pick up my jacket from the kitchen table and there they are. Just sitting there. The keys.

I'm not sure I'm safe in a car any more. I was teased so relentlessly when I learnt to drive that my confidence was seriously damaged. Now it has drained away. I feel like one of those flags you see in the side chapel of a church – once adorning a tank, or some armed militia and now ragged, threadbare and shot through with bullet holes. Every single journey I make in London, I find myself in Regent's Park, wondering where on earth I am going. It's not long since I drove the wrong way down a one-way street and came radiator to radiator with a very cross person.

I said I was very sorry. He said that wasn't good enough.

Who was it who wrote, 'Hell is a city much like London'?

Someone on the Melvyn Bragg programme this morning gave me pause by talking about Andromache and putting stress on the penultimate syllable. Andro*mach*e.

'I knew Andrew Mackie,' Mother said. 'Nice boy.'

She was powdering her nose at the time with some really orange Max Factor pancake stuff *circa* 1940. She got most of it on one side of her nose and the rest on her specs.

We're a bit forlorn this week, really. Both of us are missing Em about the place. We cheer up in the evening. The bar opens earlier than it should, these days, when it's dark so early. We get restless around five p.m. Dr Wilkie said he thought Ma might be a bit dehydrated, so I put more tonic in her gin. This weather, she is rather partial to a brandy and ginger ale. In pub terms, she probably knocks back a triple. Uncle Arthur got rid of the pub measure ages ago. 'Your mother says it barely wets the bottom of the glass,' he said.

I perk up when I'm inventing supper with a dainty aperitif. Ma sits with her feet up on her Recamier couch listening to the radio. I fossick about in the kitchen setting the table, making lists and listening to the radio. If Delia Smith's on TV our evening is made; we haven't got much further with *Little Dorrit*.

I get to bed early and read, which is heaven. Otherwise I feel a bit beached. Like being on a desert island unexpectedly. Beautiful and empty. I feel I must take up a hobby. Learn something. French is top of the list. I'll be given the Bible and *The Complete Works of Shakespeare*, of course, but I think on a lighter note I'd like a book of rumpty-tumpty poems. Long ones. With stories that rhyme. Easier to learn and cheering for the soul while waiting for the rescue or when taken hostage by Johnny Depp.

Those chaps who were made to learn poems by the yard as a punishment for missed prep or chucking bread rolls at each other won't know how lucky they are till they're stuck on an island or held hostage. I wouldn't mind knowing the whole of *The Highwayman* whose 'breeches ... fitted with never a wrinkle' and who was 'shot ... like a dog on the highway ... with a bunch of lace at his throat'. I like a STORY.

I may just order Palgrave's *Golden Treasury* at Bookpoint in Dunoon.

Went to tell Ma supper was ready and she was snoozing on her couch, empty glass in her hand.

When I called her she had no idea where she was, who she was, or who or what I was.

Gradually surfacing, she said, 'I think I may have been a little bit nearly dead.'

'a little bit, nearly dead'

Edgar and Joan came over the water on Saturday and Ma made a trifle. All week. It was a bit like a class in primary school. She used everything. Sandra Primrose from Sunnyside came in and viewed the result. 'What's that you've decorated it with?' I heard her ask.

'That's a kiwi fruit,' Ma said, like a primary school teacher. 'Those wee furry things.' She had sliced up a small potato.

Thing about Ma, though, is that she found it funnier than anyone. She wheezed for ages as we picked the slices out of the cream topping. I told her the story about the actor Peter Bull, who decorated a trifle with some really nice-looking items from the fridge. They were suppositories.

———————

What is it about mugs? We had eight at least. I can find only five. I know I haven't broken any. It's like socks. Why have I always got odd socks? We have no washing machine to search and I've explored down the legs of my spare jeans. Nothing.

Went to the Bothy and found one mug on the floor by the bunk bed and one in the sink. That's seven. One mug to go. It'll be in the garden. Full of rain.

The next mystery was a wee muslin bag Marianne found under Mego's bed. It seemed to be full of pebbles or offcuts from a small tree. Opening it very gingerly, we discovered corks. Ancient discoloured corks. Mego thought I was offering her a sweetie when I showed her what we'd found and looked so thrilled. I'll have to buy some tomorrow.

'But they're corks, Ma,' I said.

'CORKS! Why are you offering me a cork?'

At last she remembered. 'I keep a bag of corks in the bed and it stops me having cramp.'

'And does it?'

'Certainly it does. I haven't had cramp for years.'

The corks looked as if they'd been on the floor for years.

'If you get cramp,' I said, 'maybe you should have a banana before you go to bed.'

'A banana!' Ma yelped. 'I've never heard of anything so ridiculous.'

'Tennis players eat them between sets.'

'TENNIS PLAYERS! I never play tennis.'

'They get cramp so they eat them for potassium. Maybe you need potassium.'

'What I need is a large drink.'

It was eleven in the morning. We had coffee. Mind you, it was an idea.

———•———

Mother woke last night about three a.m. and called, 'Yoo-hoo. Anyone home? What's for breakfast?'

I slithered downstairs to tell her it was three a.m.

She seemed to be fiddling with her radio, so I asked if she'd like it on. She said, no, she was just trying to make herself a piece of toast.

Something made me lock the front door as I went back to bed.

———•———

Found on the flyleaf of a book I got at the Oxfam shop in Hillfoot Street: 'The best of life is life lived quietly where nothing happens but our calm journey thru' the day, where change is imperceptible and the precious life is everything,' J. McGahern.

He'll be Irish.

———•———

We've been to the hairdresser. Ma looks as if she has been electrocuted. I believe it's known as a light perm.

We are still novices with the shower and if we don't get the ghastly shower cap on properly she ends up looking special-needs and I have to do pin curls and scorch her with that dodgy hairdryer. Best thing is that she gets an outing and they are lovely to her at the Beauty Box.

Driving home we passed the ruins of that tiny old hotel on the shores of the loch called something dotty like the Drop Inn. Mother said in magisterial tones: 'Lovely little place. Nice to see them doing so well.' She suggested we call in there for lunch next time we're in town. 'That's something to look forward to,' she said.

It's a shell. Fire ripped through it, blackening the stone round the windows and splintering the slated roof, leaving it open to the skies. It must have been fierce.

I'm suddenly grateful that we have an electric stove at the cottage, even though I don't understand it. I'm terrified of fire. Sophie called into my flat one day when I was up here and smelt the faintest trace of woodsmoke. Calling to collect the post that evening, she saw it. A pale curl of blue smoke floating up from the wooden sill. The sun had fixed its gaze on my magnifying glass and was about to set the window sill on fire. Just one spark would have ignited the mess of papers on what's known as my in-tray.

Tony Hopkins's wife set her bedroom on fire twice with her make-up mirror. The firemen said it was a common occurrence.

Oh, and what about that chicken dish? That was shaming. I had cooked a delicious *coq au vin* for an American friend the day before I flew up to the cottage and I left the remains in the oven. It was summer time. Sophie, in her role as caretaker, was alerted by a shocking smell coming through the letterbox. My Le Creuset was crawling.

———

Mother, invigorated by her morning in town, has now renewed plans to visit her old sweetheart, Jack Chown, in Australia.

It's a tribute to her spirit, actually.

I still haven't told her he's dead.

———

Alzheimer's, senile dementia, dementia. What's the difference? Not much for the carer. Ma is just a confused old person. And is it hereditary, genetic, whatever you call it? Oh dear. If someone told me I had Alzheimer's, I'd lose hope. 'Sticks and stones,' we chanted as children, 'may break my bones, but words will never hurt me.' Such rubbish.

I didn't sleep till first light as Ma woke every hour yoo-hooing and banging about. I rang Mildew when she had finally dropped off.

'At least you're not required to sing war songs like Mrs Hakes's daughter,' she said. '"Wish Me Luck As You Wave Me Goodbye" is one of her favourites, varied occasionally with "We don't want to lose you but we think you ought to go".'

Her latest complaint is that her panty-liners make her very uncomfortable. Apparently she sticks them the wrong way up so that they attach themselves to her fuzzy bits. D'you see? We shrieked.

Mildew said I must ring the doctor. Again. I don't ask the right questions. I am to write them down. What exactly is her medication? If she's taking little blue pills called 'haloperidol' I am to take them away from her. 'Don't throw them down the loo, Drear. Send them to me.' Honestly. But I will definitely ring the doctor today and ask him to call when he's in the vicinity. Ma's odd behaviour is so intermittent I get lulled, but I will ring.

I cleaned the stove.

It helped.

I'm going to make Spanish onions for supper to cheer up our sausages. I'll ring the doctor first.

'Stick' or is it 'nail' or maybe 'screw' 'your courage to the sticking place'? That's him again. It'll be the old unmentionable. We're a superstitious lot on the boards. If you quote the wicked Scottish play backstage there's hell to pay. 'Angels and ministers of God defend us,' people yelp. And if you whistle in the dressing room you have to swear violently, leave the room, turn round three times and knock for re-admittance. The origin of that? Fly-men were often ex-sailors used to rigging sails on a whistled command so there was a real danger of lowering scenery on to a star. I knew a stage manager who lowered the front tabs on Donald Wolfit and lived to tell the tale.

SPANISH ONIONS

6 tbsp olive oil
2 lbs wee onions thickly sliced
2 oz seedless raisins
4 fl. oz white wine
Salt

Heat oil in a heavy pan. Add all and cook slowly for an hour or more.

———————

They don't tell you when they're coming, do they, doctors? We were on the *qui vive* all morning, expecting his call. We were clean and tidy. I had a major call of nature, much overdue, and Mother was shouting, 'DOOR! DOOR!' The phone was ringing and I still hadn't sorted the flood in the kitchen after our morning shower, so I arrived at the door with wet hands, brandishing a mop and my shirt half out of my waistband, only to find the doctor comfortably installed beside Ma, having a lovely time. She couldn't have been more delightful and gracious, and there wasn't a scintilla of a sign of muddled behaviour. Nothing about her seemed in any way other than perfectly fine. Mind you, she did keep asking about her next appointment with Dr Fezackerly. That's what he's called now – Mr Escalope is off the menu.

We are to get news next week. Otherwise it was a huge anti-climax. Except for Mother. It made her day.

———

Good phone call from the doctor.

He had diagnosed *me* very accurately. I knew I looked mad. Anyway, he is sending the district nurse in once a week to give Ma a shower and check on her medicaments. I'm thrilled. When Marianne came I shot into town for a few items, a newspaper and a wee exercise book for notes re Ma's medicines, blood pressure and such. It meant I'd get a good half-hour for a walk. I could just throw myself up the path to Blawearie or onto the Laird's Grave and back again.

Em rang from New York and I took her call in the parlour. When I got back into the sitting room there was no sign of Mego. She had got bored and, looking for me, had pulled back the curtains and was trying to exit through the window.

It threw her rather.

Huge day today. I cleaned the shower within an inch of its life, sorted out the best towels, hung up the soap-on-a-rope, having rinsed it carefully of grubby suds from my gardening hands, laid out the best talc (Penhaligon's Bluebell), a facecloth and sponge and that scratchy thing Ma likes for her back. I even put the shampoo alongside, just in case. Hung her dress- ing-gown and shower cap on the door and, in a state of sweet anticipation, placed my walking boots in the porch.

Nursie came well after the appointed hour, so I filled in time fussing with a pretty plate of shortbread biscuits and grinding good coffee beans in Ma's old box machine.

Ma, by this time, was up to high-do and watching at the sitting-room window.

Well, Nursie came. Nice. Not a load of laughs. Introductions were made. Ma was lovely and asked her to sit down and have a drink. Fearful that she was about to offer a G and T, I said I was making coffee and did she take milk and sugar. She said neither. She wasn't stopping. They were under pressure from a time-and-motion study and she had an elderly gent in Kilmun to fit in. I said I'd run the shower immediately and she said she wouldn't manage it this visit. Maybe next week, and would I be available as they are not allowed to shower any patient on their own? Health and safety, you know!

I'm going to bomb them when I'm Queen.

Quite a good night and a glorious morning. I spent
an hour or so fixing Emily Gray to the gable end.
The high winds last week ripped her off her fixings.
I couldn't find any wire so I cut some old tights
into strips and I think it'll hold. The sun was really
quite warm on my back. Not a midge within miles.
Mildew was so badly bitten by clegs and midges last
August she said she thought she could be cremated
for half-price. Jimmie Helm says they only live for
a day and it's not a great career, is it?

As the poem says,

it'skin' o
thankless
didje
ever
spen
a
hail simmer
stottin
up
an
doon.

I put out Ma's chair and collected a couple of rugs thinking she could sit outside for a treat, but by the time I'd got her up and ready, black clouds had banked over Gourock and Marianne said rain was forecast. We did a short walk instead, but out of the sun it was chilly so we turned back at the corner. Ma looked balefully at the steps up to the garden and said authoritatively, 'I don't think I should be doing stairs today.'

I brewed the coffee I'd ground for Nursie and finished my breakfast toast, which I found on the

mantelpiece. I knew I hadn't finished it. My stomach has a very good memory.

Nurse number two called today and we got 'fell in' for our shower. There was wee Mego naked and nervous under a dribbling shower and big Nurse just alongside, as it were, making free with a flannel and avoiding getting wet. And there's me stood standing, like a parking attendant, with a towel and a dressing-gown, making inane conversation. 'They also serve who only stand and wait.'

Well, we got Mego gowned up and sat at the window to recover while Nursie wrote the date in our notebook. I suppose just to indicate that she had called. Her visit simply doesn't include tea and a chat with the patient, when it strikes me this would be the best medicine.

No walk today.

Marianne bounced in with thrilling gossip. Ma was always talking about that mysterious doctor who, it was rumoured, purveyed illicit substances to the upper classes. I once saw him looking rather shifty coming out of the gents' loo in West Hampstead. Nothing upper class round there, surely.

However, he is apparently staying at the hotel across the road. Thrilling indeed.

He comes into the bar most nights, so he has struck up an acquaintance with Mr Menzies, sitting in his usual corner. He has one of those domed bald heads with a couple of bumps on it. He couldn't get his cap on.

he couldn't get his cap on.

Well, Dr P cut a slit in a page from his copy of *The Times*, put it over Mr M's head, gave him a whisky and cut them out. It's very successful. Apparently. I wondered if he'd administered marijuana as a form of anaesthetic ... I mean, did he stitch up the wounds?

I'd heard long since that marijuana is good for glaucoma. I wish I had the courage to contact Dr P. Just chat to him in the bar and ask for a spliff or a joint or a stash or whatever it's called. I mean, is it illegal if you are nearly ninety? Who cares? Mego loved a Passing Cloud in the old days. When she gets a bit blue of an evening she could sit at her window puffing on a joint and letting life flow gently by. It would be a marvellous Christmas present. The other evening she suddenly said, in tragic tones, 'Phyllida, why have you brought me here?'

I spent an agonising half-hour explaining as gently as I could where we were and that it was her home. I relived the move from the manse but that made matters worse. 'No, no, Phyllida, I know the manse, that's not where I mean.' By the end I got out of it with a nice drink and a promise to take her out tomorrow, if the weather is kind, and we'll look for her house. She says she'll know it as soon as she sees it. Nightmare. What if I have to evict someone? Was it the full moon? I believe it's supposed to have a disturbing effect on the elderly.

Go to bed and sob.

Miserable raw day. I thought Ma might have forgotten yesterday but as we sat down to lunch (soup) she asked when we were going to look for 'it'. She was very gentle and polite with me, despite, or perhaps because of, the fact that I was clearly to blame for her situation. I tried to distract her by talking wildly about the dreadful Dr P, the blocked stove-pipe, the price of eggs. Anything. Useless. She wouldn't rest after lunch today: she wanted to see her house while it was still light. She knew just where it was. I asked if we should take the car, but she said, 'Not at all. We can see it from the road.'

I got her into Uncle Arthur's old brown Puffa jacket, found her stick and off we went. I was convinced she was thinking of the old manse, so I turned right at the gate, but Ma went left, and walked determinedly past the hotel and towards the tea-rooms. I wondered if the tea-rooms might be what she meant, but 'No, no, Phyllida. I know the tea-rooms,' and on we went, a little hesitant now, and stopping, to my horror, in front of Blink-bonny. The thought of a confrontation with old Mrs Bathgate loomed, but after a puzzled little wander and a short stop at the church, she turned back, saying it was cold, 'it' wasn't here and 'We'll try again tomorrow.'

'There's a suitcase behind the door that we have to pick up. Arthur needs it,' she said.

I lit the fire in the sitting room, switched the TV on for company and went to put the kettle on. When I went back with a cup of sweet lemon tea, she said, 'Take my curlers out, dear. I have a feeling George wants us all in church.'

Who, for Heaven's sake, is George?

———

Phone call from Soph. Her wheat allergy is official. It has been confirmed. She has taken all the tests. Her homeopath says it runs in families so we should all take the tests. What fun. Just the sort of thing I enjoy. By odd coincidence, I heard one of those cheerful radio programmes on good health that always give me a sharp attack of hypochondria. The doctor, who sounded like a nice young man, said an allergy to wheat was linked to eczema and schizophrenia. Dementia and schizophrenia under one roof. Lovely.

As it happens, Soph and I have both had eczema and she did once ring me up and ask if there was any madness in the family. I never got to the bottom of that. And I do talk to myself.

And I wander the cottage in all directions, looking for the mug of tea I just put down. 'What you haven't got in your head you'd better keep in your feet!'

Miserable night again.

Found Mego, in her flannel nightie and no slippers, looking puzzled and anxious, wandering round the parlour with her toothbrush in her hand. 'Phyllida, someone has taken the basin.' Got her back to bed but she was calling out for breakfast around five a.m.

She clearly wasn't going to settle to sleep so we had a sort of breakfast at six, got her dressed, and she was seated at the window by seven, anxious now because it was so dark. I risked a shower to wake me up.

I've been in denial, haven't I? She really has left the building.

Someone has taken the fascin

It's just that she has always been dotty. Delicious dotty. Crackers, scatty, nutty, nuts, bananas, batty, bats, cuckoo, barmy, bonkers, potty, dotty, wacky – all of those listed in *Roget's Thesaurus*. I once got one of her letters signed, 'Yours faithfully, Margaret C. Law', while the butcher got one signed 'With love and kisses, darling, Ma'. And didn't we all love it when she sent a May bug to the Forestry Commission in a matchbox because she thought it was a Colorado beetle.

But, tucked in among the dottiness, she was wise. 'Don't waste your time trying to be perfect,' she would say. '*L'idiot savant*. Just a minute, should that be feminine? *L'idiote savante*? Surely not. And isn't *savant* soap? No. That's *savon*.'

My ambition regarding French is very tattered. I've read Harry Potter in French but it'll be a while before I hit Flaubert.

I'll speak to the nurse who will tell me to speak to the doctor. I spoke to Mildew. She said it sounded like her medication. She says Fred Spooner was diagnosed HIV positive, but he says he took Boots multi-vitamins and it went away. I'll buy some.

On a quick visit to town, while Marianne gave Ma tea and sympathy, an approaching lorry and two cars flashed me meaningfully and I thought, Oo-er, it's the fuzz, but no. When I turned the corner I met a swan. There was quite a queue of traffic on the other lane, waiting for her to make up her mind to move.

Who was it who was driving in the country when a red-faced woman lowered her window and yelled 'PIG' at him? He lowered his window and yelled 'COW' before turning the corner and hitting a pig.

———·——

I've been in such a state it was easy to ring the doctor. I don't quite know how it happened but I was rude to Ma, and she had a little dry sob as she trotted along the yellow duct tape that takes her through the parlour to the loo, like a miserable child. And then she trotted back, bravely pretending to be cheerful. That finished me.

It's devastating to watch your mother weep. Mego was a stoic and I saw her sob only twice.

The worst time was when we had visited my brother in hospital the day before an operation on his head. A serious-looking nursing sister handed Mother a little printed card, which she tucked into her handbag. On the bus home she took it out to read. It stated that she was allowed the special right to visit outside hours in view of the extreme seriousness of the patient's condition. She put the card neatly back into her handbag and started very gently, almost imperceptibly, to weep like a small child without hope of comfort. When James died twenty-five years later I never saw her weep. I knew her pillow was wet and I saw her face drained of light.

'Those are pebbles that were her eyes.'

You see, I'm weeping now. It's ridiculous. Touch me and I leak tears. Grief, like arsenic, stays in the system where we store all the unshed tears from long-ago life. Some things are too terrible for tears so we keep them for later, and they surface at odd and often inopportune moments.

The sound of applause on the radio can make me weep, the sound of a steam train, Paul Robeson singing 'lulalulabyebye', gentle English countryside seen from a train window, or somebody's little square house in a field with the lights on. It's embarrassing because it's trivial. Soph caught me sobbing and whimpering one Christmas when my brandy snaps didn't work. She has hated them ever since.

In the 'too terrible' category, I wring my hands. It's a cliché I couldn't use on stage. I actually pace up and down and wring my hands. Interesting.

A lovely elderly actor I worked with told me his kitchen once caught fire and, standing in the doorway, stunned, he noted that his hands did not fly upwards, in the stock response to shock, but dropped slowly downwards to his sides. Even in that emergency he marked it down for use.

Why could I not apologise, say I was sorry and ashamed and hug Ma till she squeaked? I simply couldn't. How graceless. Maybe you have to be taught to hug.

I blame boarding school.

I blame being an evacuee.

I blame the war.

I wonder if there are other damaged goods like me. I don't hug. My daughters do. Indeed, they sometimes hug me and say it's like hugging an 'offended umbrella'. They tell me I am 'unopened'. I tell them it's generational. I tell them it's my upbringing. I tell them I'm Scottish. Their grandmother, Mego, didn't approve of people holding hands in the street.

———

I wish I had been better at talking to Ma, questioning her, finding out about her life, but I think she was as secretive as I am. The girls were really bold with their enquiries. I had been known to hide behind the sitting-room door to listen. If there were lots of wheezing hysterics, I knew they were on to men, sex and indecent limericks.

Little Willie in the best of sashes
Fell in fire and was burnt to ashes.
Later, when the room grew chilly
Nobody like to poke poor Willy.

Or

Aunty Mary had a canary
Up the leg o' her drawers.
She pu'd a string,
Tae mak it sing
An' doon cam Santy Claus.
For hoors and hoors, it cursed the Boers.
And it won the Victoria Cross.

The doctor visited again. He said it was all his fault: the medication he prescribed had given Mego drug-induced Parkinson's, which is why she has that permanently anxious look. I just thought she was permanently anxious.

Mildew did a bit of research and tells me Dime-a-box is used as a medicine for altitude sickness, which seems weird. Ma can barely manage the garden steps. Dr W says it's to control her glaucoma and Dr Sack-of-bits is looking up dosage to review her prescription. Diagnosis must be fascinating for doctors, if confusing for the patient. Are we called that because we have to be? Patient? Trouble is, I never ask the right questions. No wonder I don't get much in the way of answers.

Dr W suggests that she goes into the geriatric ward for a week so that we can sort it out. He was convincingly apologetic and said he'd managed to poison Dorothy-next-door as well. Ma will be sorted out soon, he said, and why don't I skip home to London for a day or two when I have the chance?

So, I'm going. I'll take Ma into hospital on Tuesday morning, settle her in and then catch a ferry around teatime. She seems to be looking forward to what she calls a 'holiday' and I am a bag of nerves. Well, at least she'll have a holiday from me. I'll manage to see the girls, check on the flat and leave it ready for Bunny, coming over from Canada. He's looking for work here. Sounds dodgy, but it'll be nice to know the flat is kept warm.

I bet the boiler goes on the blink.

———

The boiler did. Go on the blink. Timing? Bunny is due next week. I hope he'll be all right in my narrow hospital bed. Who was it who called my bedroom that of a 'racy nun'? It'll be the lace curtain I use as a coverlet.

Got lots done, including Penhaligon's for Ma's Christmas present. Em and Ken are hoping to film *Much Ado About Nothing* in early spring. It's been on the cards since *Peter's Friends*.

Sophie has got a long weekend at Christmas, but I have put my feet down. Every flight, every freight train will be full. Gone are those dramatic overnight drives through snow-covered hills – for the moment, anyway.

Caught a later ferry than I'd hoped. I saw the four-fifteen leave the pier just as I got to the Cloch lighthouse. I'd have caught it, had I not spent ages in the car park at the airport looking for my car. Of course I thought it had been stolen and felt sick, but I was on the wrong floor.

Still had time to whip into the geri ward to see Ma and give her fair warning of her move home tomorrow. Sister McKee thinks the change in her medication will be helpful. When she came in to say hello and goodbye Ma said, 'How do you do and who are you, dear?'

'I'm Sister McKee,' she said.

'Mr McKee?' asked Ma.

'No! I'm a sister.'

'My sister?' said Ma.

'No, no I'm a nurse.'

'I never knew that. Where do you work now?'

Wishing to disentangle herself Sister McKee changed the subject. 'Isn't it nice to see Phyllida?'

'See Phyllida! Fat chance,' said Ma.

I'm picking her up at eleven tomorrow morning.

Dumped bags in the parlour. Cottage peaceful and sweet-smelling. Marianne has been, of course. Made a quick snack of toasted cheese for 'tea', using Ma's old trick of spreading it with marmalade and grilling it till it browned and bubbled. Heaven. How do Americans manage without a proper grill? Unpacked all over the floor and rang everyone. It's been a wonderful trip, really. Which brings me to –

THE BAD ONE

Someone who shall be nameless had heard my constant cry for marijuana to alleviate Ma's glaucoma and had not only availed themselves of some, but had taken it into account that I was to try it first before experimenting on Mother. A tea-party was arranged to include baked items as I can't and never have smoked or inhaled or anything. If I have to smoke onstage, I usually bend the bloody thing or wet it down to the lit end and choke.

I decided to bake scones and sprinkled some of the revolting-looking compost into my mixture along with the usual sugar and pinch of salt. My overseers said that the amount I had sprinkled was barely a fagful. 'There are five of us,' they pointed out, as they spooned in a ladleful. I provided cream and bramble jelly and the scones came out of the oven looking perfectly innocent.

Well, they weren't.

They tasted delicious and at first nothing occurred. We could have been the Women's Institute. People started to giggle a lot, got boring and went home. I can't remember in what order.

I don't know how long it took me to know that I was going to die.

I remember thinking it was a pity.

I remember thinking I had ruined everyone's life.

I remember trying to throw up and failing.

I remember watching the water I threw on my face gurgling down the plughole for what seemed like hours. I thought, I bet time has stopped. I've probably only been here for seconds. My brain was oddly clear, but the perspectives in my flat had skewed dramatically. The walls tipped, the floor moved. It was like being on a yacht pitching in heavy seas round Cape Horn.

I called a co-conspirator to say I was dying.

I'm told I lay on my narrow hospital bed with my hands crossed neatly on my breast, like one of those effigies on tombs in cathedrals, intoning repeated instructions about where to find my will: 'Bottom right-hand drawer of the desk,' I chanted.

A doctor was called and a lot of strangers wandered in and out of my bedroom with hot sweet tea. Meanwhile, though dying, I took a forensic interest in my symptoms and the doctor's pink shirt. He told me I wasn't dying and rang some hospital to check on procedure.

'I have a patient here having a bad trip,' I heard him say. I knew better.

Having glared at the chastened company over his bifocals, he simply asked in headmasterly tones, 'WHY?' and left to collect his medical bag. From this he produced a giant-sized syringe full of some turquoise liquid, which he injected into my bottom. I believe every detail will be in his notes. How shaming. It was supposed to make me sleep, but it didn't. I reflected that I had been, as Mother said, 'A little bit nearly dead', and waited, fully clothed, for the morning.

I think I am still 'chilled out'. I think that's the phrase. Or is it 'spaced'? (I have moved into 'yoof' culture, but I don't have to stay.) They tell me marijuana remains in your system for months. I can certainly vouch for the fact that it's with me now. At Heathrow, I picked up a charming ancient Indian person who was lost and very nearly took him to Pakistan. Well, at least I got him to the correct gate before I calmly returned for my standby ticket and for the very first time had to wait for the next plane. I was totally serene about the whole experience, which is quite out of character. This would be perfect for Mego. It's a great pity we got it wrong and she won't benefit.

Bed now.

District nurse coming. So is Christmas. Ma has started emptying her jewellery box onto the bed almost every day and sorting through all the wee things she has. She wants to give her onyx pinkie ring to Sophie for Christmas, the Victorian mourning brooch to Emma. It has a tiny plait of blonde hair at the back. Rather spooky. Hair doesn't change colour when we're dead, does it?

'Does Tootsiekamoon still have her hair?' Ma wonders, as she lays everything out on her coverlet.

She is very happy making lists. The doctor always gets a tin of biscuits, apparently. Fox's assorted. Delivered. Then there's Dorothy-next-door, Beggsie, Marianne, Mrs Lees, Mrs Grey, the lady at the garage, Mrs Delmahoy and that nice lady who wears hats and keeps a flamingo, the one who colours her hair with rug dye, and who is the one who knits? It keeps her occupied. So does the mincemeat I bought under instruction (cheat, Phyllida, cheat). A large pot has been decanted into the biggest bowl in the kitchen for Ma to stir and add grated carrots, sharp apples, real suet and a slug or two of booze (more, Phyllida, more).

We've got new horse pills. I hope they work.

'I come from haunts of coot and hern,' said Mother.

'Did you make a sudden sally?' I asked. I was cleaning the hearth.

'Fat chance. Haven't seen her for years,' she said.

We actually made pastry this morning. It was a bold decision. We flung it everywhere. Ma always lifts her pastry mix up high and lets it drop from a great height to 'let the air in, Phyllida'. It quite often hits the bowl but it can land in some rather unexpected places. Meanwhile she whistles under her breath and waves her wee hands around, announcing that one is either a cook or a baker, not both, and that I am very heavy-handed. True. Nevertheless I have collected quite a lot of it and it's in the fridge. Resting. Since the oven is on high for our baked potatoes tonight, I'll make a few mince pies for a treat. Nice to be ahead of ourselves.

Postscript: the pastry was alarmingly short and the pies had to be patched. I sieved icing sugar over them as decoration and disguise. They tasted odd. A quick sniff and a lick and I realised I'd sieved flour instead of icing sugar.

'Lovely, dear,' Mego said.

WALNUT SLICE

6 oz self-raising flour
4 oz margarine
8 oz sugar
apricot jam
2 egg whites
4 oz broken walnuts

Rub fat into flour and sugar. Using a little milk mix into a dough. Press into a baking tin and bake in a moderate oven. Spread with apricot jam. Into a pan put the egg whites, the rest of the sugar and the broken walnuts. Bring slowly to the boil, stirring till golden and fluffy. Spread over the pastry and bake till golden in a moderate oven.

This went down very well, and it triggered a few useful memories although the walnut pieces made Ma's teeth wobble a bit. I tried to weasel out the details of her famous pineapple cakes but being a natural cook, she'd just thrown them together and now she has no idea how. 'Lots of cream and butter icing, dear,' she said, waving a royal hand.

But she did remember how the tour buses lined the village street 'from the church to the Hotel', and people in hats picked all the flowers in Miss Niven's window boxes. One bus driver always filled his top pocket with pancakes warm off the griddle.

———·——

Today I got really ratty because Mother kept complaining that her morning tea was perfectly disgusting. 'It's like medicine,' she kept repeating, 'just like medicine.'

I stumped off to get her a fresh cup telling her that it was probably her 'vitamins' that were making her tea taste odd, only to discover that Marianne had cleaned the mugs and the teapot yesterday by soaking them in a solution of bleach.

Fondly remembered are the old actor who arrived early for rehearsal one day and the stage manager who asked him if he'd like a tea or coffee. 'I think I'll have a gin and Domestos,' he said. When she came back with his cup of tea he was dead.

Lovely last words.

———•◦•———

Stores to cover the holiday are nearly complete. A case of wine from the kids was delivered yesterday. Mego said it looked as if we were running a small hotel. Huge, lumpy parcel from Soph: two Christmas stockings filled with tiny packages carefully wrapped and beribboned. One for Mego, one for me. This, despite my admonishments. No presents this year. We are going to build our day round the carols from King's College, Cambridge,

and our New Year round the concert from Vienna. Quite enough.

The weather has suddenly closed in with vicious night frosts turning the sodden garden path into the Cresta Run. I put my crampons on and took a torch to deliver the odd Christmas card. Gertie Mackay is in a state about her electricity bill. She bought a nice wee two-bar electric fire because Dougie was feeling the cold and the walls were 'condescending' – 'But it was a stretch, Mrs Thompson, and I never knew there was extra to pay on the top of it.'

Last time we had a spell like this the water supply froze and we had a water-van and a stand-pipe on the shore road. I think I'll fill the bath.

———•———

Later: we haven't got a bath.

———•———

The frost has really taken hold. When I went to shut the porch doors tonight the stars were Hollywood bright. I was staring at one that looked particularly green, when I realised the sky around it was pulsing. A delicate and ragged curtain of pink and green kept dripping and sliding down to touch the hills and then fade upwards.

The Northern Lights.

The Aurora Borealis.

I've never seen them before. I spent about two hours rushing from the front of the cottage to the back because the whole sky seemed to be breathing. Staring upwards made my neck hurt and I started to shiver.

O God, make small the old star-eaten blanket of
  the sky
That I may wrap it round me and in comfort lie.

I learnt that on the Jubilee Line. *Poems on the Underground.* Can't remember the rest.

Felt rather weepy. Made a hot-water bottle and went unwillingly to bed.

What a wonderful Christmas present.

Wish Ma could have seen it.

---

1 JANUARY 1994

New Year Resolution. I am going to put dates in my diary.

Ma and I managed to ignore Christmas. It was really peaceful. She still wants to find her 'house', but she seems to realise it's not convenient at this time of year. There was a disturbing moment when she wondered how Arthur was managing in the cupboard, and I'm always a bit anxious at dusk watching her mind slip into the dark. Good moment too. At the end of the Viennese concert, she suddenly said, 'Phyllida, what's that thing on the end of my leg?'

'It's your foot, Mother.'

She seemed appalled.

We were both ready for bed early on New Year's Eve so that was fine, but in spite of everything I couldn't sleep and I heard the mournful midnight hooting of the ships on the Clyde. I don't think I got to sleep till about four a.m.

I wouldn't mind so much if any thoughts I had between two and five a.m. were of any use. I wouldn't mind being an insomniac if it produced results. It did for Bernard Levin.

Didn't he get Alzheimer's? Such a brilliant man, with a genius for incredibly long sentences. He once gave me a bad notice for playing Mistress Overdone, the brothel-keeper in *Measure for Measure*, with a Glasgow accent.

I still think it was a good idea.

Phone call. Thought it would be the girls. A transatlantic voice said, 'Congratulations. You have been randomly selected to have a holiday in Florida. To hear more details press nine.' I rang off. Minutes later the phone rang again. 'I don't want a holiday in Florida,' I snapped. It was Mike Newell offering me a job.

It's remarkably easy to say no when it is quite simply out of the question. There's very little anguish involved. Besides which, I haven't read the script. A good script is a rare temptation and might make it painful.

7 JANUARY

Things are moving now. The holiday is over. The phone is getting busy. Could I play a nun in a film about Beethoven? A nun. I'd love to play a nun. Would I have a wimple? And would I get to meet Beethoven? Then my agent said it was in Budapest. I declined. She rang back. It's only two little scenes, which would shoot in a week with fixed dates. Good pay.

Just a week in Budapest. I wonder if there's a direct flight from Glasgow.

———·—·———

8 JANUARY

Awful night again. Ma has now developed a snore that sounds as if she is calling me.

'Phy … lli … daaaah.'

So I get to be awake even when she's asleep.

———·—·———

9 JANUARY

Thing is, you see, my Christmas present from Em is a bank account in Dunoon that would cover another Golden Girl, or maybe even two? No one should do two nights in a row. It was quite good when Ma's drugs were reviewed a while back, but last night she woke at twelve thirty, three a.m and five forty-five. I'm noting it down and so is Beggsie. She's having a hard time reassuring Mother about her 'house'. She had to call Dorothy-next-door, Jim Thomas, and the Primroses when I was in Glasgow and no one could settle Mother. Till her whisky and ginger ale. Word has got round the coast, though, and a sweet-sounding woman called Mary is coming to tea to look us over. She might give us a trial run this week. Must spread ash on the Cresta Run.

Apparently there is yet another Mary at Benmore who might do the odd night.

'Mary Beaton and Mary Seton and Mary Carmichael and me.'

Years ago I was in a play about Mary Queen of Scots at the Edinburgh Festival.

I played one of the Marys, doubling it with an extremely ancient servant to the ailing James I. I remember shuffling across the stage in a lot of hefty padding and a mob cap, carrying a tankard of some noxious liquid made of gravy browning and saying in a strong Scots accent: 'Here is yer potion,

Yer Majesty.' They were the first words I spoke on any stage. A triumph.

The costumes were great, actually. They were produced by Motley Theatre Design, with spectacular ruffs made of milliner's scrim, and the blokes wore a lot of chains: when Darnley came courting the Queen and knelt at her feet, he sounded like a train shunting into a siding. In an adjoining space we did a late-night cabaret afterwards, serving hot dogs. Just as Queen Mary was coping with the last rites and our star, Catherine Lacey, had uttered

here is yer potion yer majesty --

the immortal words, 'Melville, I leave my last cares in your truss ...' (she never put a T on the end), the ceiling fell in next door. We still did the cabaret, though.

---

17 JANUARY

Finally rang doctor. He said one word: 'Go'.

---

31 JANUARY

I'm doing it.

---

4 FEBRUARY

Packed and ready, up London.

5 FEBRUARY

I know the second assistant director on this film. He's great. He rang up to give me my travel 'movement', like they do, with all those troublesome e-tickets and reference numbers. Why can't I just have a wee bit of paper that I can lose, like I used to? Anyway, Alex and I had a shriek on the telephone and my 'pick-up' was to be a very civilised nine thirty a.m. and the driver would have all the necessary info. I'd be met at the other end, of course, and I'd see him for a drink at the hotel. Fine. Looking forward. Yeah, yeah. Know the score.

Morning came, car arrived, off we went. Got into Heathrow's Terminal 4. No sign of a flight to Budapest. Nice official said I was in the wrong terminal. Took a cab to Terminal 3. It took for ever and cost arms and legs. Very odd. They had a seat, no problem, but I'd have to run for it. Paid up personally and got pushed through a side door to get to the gate fast and my luggage was thrown down a chute as I boarded.

Nice journey. No luggage. It took two hours to sort that out. No car to meet me. I took a cab, paying gleefully with some funts I'd found in my cache of foreign currency, though I'd probably have been more popular with sterling.

I couldn't wait to get a glass of wine in my hand. I'd find Alex in the hotel from where he'd rung me – he'd be in the bar and I'd find the infamous little swine and demand retribution. No one from the film company was there. I rang Alex from Reception. When he heard my voice he yelled, 'Phyllida, where are you?'

'In the bar of your hotel.'

'You're supposed to be in Vienna. I've had Interpol looking for you.'

I will never live it down.

———

A room of my own. Bliss. It's dark and peaceful. Nothing but a big bed and a bathroom. What's more, I had the whole afternoon to wander about the charming small town of Sopron. It was a two-hour drive from Budapest and half an hour from Vienna, so I grovelled to Alex and waltzed out to buy bottles of wine. One for him, one for the saintly driver and one for me. There were quite a few gift shops, of course, outside which sat a punchable doll the size of a two-year-old, padded and stitched and armed with a broomstick. Sometimes she had a witch's hat and a grim expression, but I fell for one with a toothless grin and a set of bagpipes. There must be a story behind her, like the Russian Baba Yaga, who flew around on

She seemed to have a set of bagpipes

a broomstick and had iron teeth. I can't speak any German so I don't know how to find out. I wanted to buy her but she was quite big enough to need a seat on the plane and I've caused enough trouble in that area already.

I found an antiques shop where I couldn't resist a tiny china figurine of Hitler, who looked thoroughly ashamed of himself and had 'London 1953' painted on the sole of his left boot.

The owner spoke English but she was very chilly and not keen to pass the time of day. It might have been that I wore my monocle to look at prices, then bought Hitler. She probably thought I was a Nazi.

he looked rather ashamed of himself

Filming tomorrow. No make-up required and not a lot to say. The leading man, Ed Harris, came into the make-up van with his baseball cap on backwards and said, as he passed me, 'I hear you went to Budapest.'

I said, 'Shut up.' He's nice.

Early call. I will be rushing around a thirteenth-century monastery corridor with Diane Kruger and assorted nuns.

———

I have no idea what the date is. So much for New Year resolution. Bit of a tense day. The ancient wooden flooring creaked every time the camera moved and it was difficult to get clean dialogue. I could have done with a bit of Beethoven. Apparently we are not going to get it.

I remember on a film a while ago listening to Beethoven's 'Ode to Joy' sung around midnight by a huge choir standing in deep snow halfway up the Austrian Alps. Walking back to base on a snow-encrusted path, I heard what I thought was the wind using the trees as a tuning fork. I stopped to listen and the sound grew and shifted, touched the trees and lifted, sweeping behind me. Turning, I saw that the sound man was sitting at his desk in the middle of a snowfield playing the third movement of Beethoven's Quintet 132. It hung in the air like the Aurora Borealis.

Phoned home. Joyous news. Sophie has arrived at the cottage for a few days before she starts rehearsing. I'll just miss her, of course. Double drat.

Buy salami at the airport and a tin of seductive biscuits. A very severe security person rootled around my sponge bag in a suspicious and threatening manner, finally producing a box of suppositories and waving them about. He thought they were bullets and was suitably embarrassed.

———

There's a blush for won't and a blush for shan't
And a blush for having done it.
There's a blush for thought and a blush for naught
And a blush for just begun it.
JOHN KEATS

Can you credit it?

I thought it was Aunt Ella's.

———

Managed to tuck in a supper with the company before reorganising luggage and flying home.

Casting *Much Ado* has got very Hollywood. They've got Denzel Washington for Don Pedro and are looking for a black Don John and maybe a black Ursula. I played her, I think, long years ago in Bristol, when Rosemary Harris gave her Beatrice. That must have been the time when her wee dog, a long-haired dachshund called Pinkie, ate her wig. She had forgotten to give him the comfort blanket he usually slept and played with, so he took revenge by chewing her wig, tossing it about the dressing room and clawing clumps off it to play with. There was no time to collect bits and redress it. It was a 'quick change' and she had to wear it. Actors on stage expecting her entrance had somehow to deal with the unexpected arrival of a Hottentot.

Music! hark!

282

I often wondered if the audience really noticed anything but a lot of us being unable to speak.

The kids asked if I'd be able to visit them in Tuscany but I think at the moment that's quite out of the question. Apparently their location is principally a large villa in the hills. They will be out there doing pre-production and working hard at getting a tan. The villa has a swimming-pool.

How frightful.

———•·•———

Glasgow! Such a relief to find the car sitting forlorn and dusty in the car park. Such a relief to hear the engine start.

Such a relief to get home to the cottage before dark and let Beggsie go home. She and Mother were standing in the porch waiting for me. Mother keeps repeating my name and beaming. It's touching at first and then profoundly irritating.

Because it makes me feel guilty?

———•·•———

Letter from Sophie to Emma:

I am a monstrous me
Driven to extremities by an OAP.

It is a miracle Mego is not already marinated or marmaladed or just plain gunned down. There are lots of jars in the parlour cupboard I could have fitted her in. If she mentions having to meet the bank manager one more time, or makes me count the money in her purse one more time, I will put her to bed with a live Flymo. It's almost not funny. I think I may have developed several nervous disorders.

Talking of poo, the Polaris is gone. The only visible remnant of their presence is a section of 'Marshmallow Fluff' in jars at Presto's. A fine exchange for a nuclear arsenal. In fact, I think it's 'fallout' with added sugar.

My God, it's dismal this morning.

I took my depression into the kitchen to make coffee. Rain was hammering on the coal bin outside, the noise was orchestral. Mother was, as usual, installed at her window looking bleak.

'It's as grey as a plumber's wig,' she said.

It took me a moment.

'It's a plover's wing, Mother,' I said, but it didn't half cheer me up.

———•———

OK. I think it's March and it's Wednesday. I can't do this date thing. My memory is shot to pieces. I left the electric blanket on here when I was away. That's nearly two weeks altogether.

Mary is coming tomorrow. From the case notebook, I see the nights have been pretty awful: 'Up wandering about every hour or so'; 'Lots of calling in the night. "Yoo-hoo! Anybody there? Time for breakfast"'; 'She says her teeth don't fit'; 'She needs more talc, as her legs are stuck together'; 'Her teeth hurt.'

I remember that so well with our gran.

This morning I see that Mego has her new nightie on back to front and it is far too long. Could be fun. Emma is very insistent that I should get another Golden Girl, if only for the nights. I can do weekends. We'll see how we go. Mary is coming tomorrow.

———·—·———

The days are getting longer but Ma still gets depressed around teatime. 'Be a sport, Phyllida, give me the pills.' She means Death.

I say OK, but shall we have a cup of tea first?

'Oh, yes!' she says. 'Let's have tea.'

Later on I can distract her with the offer of brandy and ginger ale.

She has asked the doctor to do 'the decent thing'. He says he can't face a prison sentence. She thinks it would make a nice change. After her evening drink she'll say wistfully, 'Old age isn't doing its duty.'

It's heartbreaking.

Words are no use. We both sit and stare at the loch. Flat. Gunmetal grey.

———•———

While Marianne was in this morning, I took a solitary drive to the local residential home to ask about extra help on a temporary basis. Perhaps just the odd night. Mother and I called there months ago to see if it was suitable for 'a little holiday' but it wasn't 'quite the thing'. However, we met this tall, rather imposing young woman called Claudia, who seemed good fun and clearly loved the job.

She is coming to tea tomorrow! May she bring her dog? Mother would love it. It's a Corgi called Ratty. Very royal.

At home, rang Mildew to get the lowdown on Corgis. They get nicked in Regent's Park, she said. One of the local dog-walkers had an Irish wolfhound everyone loved and he got his tail slammed in the car door. After the first howl, he was very cheerful, loved the fuss and wagged his bloody tail enthusiastically over everyone. Renee, the dog-walker, covered it with a condom fixed on with Elastoplast. Question: does she keep a supply of condoms in the car? Interesting.

———·—··———

This morning Mego washed her face with shampoo and brushed her hair with a toothbrush.

Rang Mildew. She says she tried to pay her newspaper account at her local Paki shop with a cheque. She asked who she should make it out to. He said, 'I gotta stamp.'

She said, 'How do you spell it?'

She shouldn't say Paki, should she? That's racist. Good grief.

———·—··———

Trotted into the sitting room to tell Ma I was off 'to town' for the messages and was there anything she needed.

'A new brain,' she said.

I told her I'd be back soon.

'OK, kid,' she said.

I think that was the first time I'd ever heard her say OK.

———•———

Claudia and Ratty have joined the team.

Pinch, punch first of the month,
Cuckoo on the hills.
Spring has sprung,
The grass is ris,
I wonder where the birdy is.
The bird is on the wing
But that's absurd.
The wing is on the bird.

———•———

Went for a trot to the postbox when Claudia arrived at teatime. Mother is calling her 'Cloth-ear'.

I was desperate for a decent walk, but the heavens opened and it was like the monsoon with extra hail. I ducked into the outside loo by the Bothy and sat down on the loo while the rain tipped down on the corrugated-iron roof. It was absolutely deafening. Perched at ease, I remembered touring 'Hindle Wakes' to a library somewhere in Devon, when hail and rain, thumping on the old tin roof, was so loud, I missed my entrance because I couldn't hear my cue. I don't suppose the audience heard the play.

Oh, and what about the opening of the Bath Music Festival when Victor de Sabata came to conduct the LPO for the inaugural concert and the hall was a purpose-built prefabricated affair with a tin roof? Well, it was hopeless. A hailstorm struck. None of the wind section could play for laughing. The gorgeous first flautist couldn't manage his embouchure, and even stern de Sabata was seen to be smiling. Princess Margaret was in the audience too.

I've scraped nearly every parked car in Greve.

I'm in Greve in Chianti.

In Tuscany.

In Italy.

In a heat wave.

What I need here is a Vespa. Ladies whiz past me, carrying hefty bags of household goods, bolt upright as if soldered to the saddle of their bike, little tin toys.

I have been shopping for *articoli da toilette*, having left my life in a carpet bag sitting on an armchair at home in London. Sponge bag, make-up, eye-drops, sketch book, pencils, pens, brushes, travelling watercolour set and, what's worse, my student's notebook.

I've done this sort of thing before, when I was decades younger and considered simply careless. On the way to the Edinburgh festival I left my entire face furniture in a lovely little pigskin case on the platform at King's Cross. Within a week my face felt like cardboard and it actually hurt to smile. A stern lady in Jenners department store was suitably outraged at this dereliction of duty and I had to fork out for assorted unguents.

I didn't worry then that I might be losing my mind. I do now. It's the sort of worry that surfaces in the February time of night between two and four a.m.

I'm writing this on the back of today's call-sheet. No call for us girls till this evening so I can just sit on this stone bench shaded by vines and get brown as directed. The heat is wonderfully crushing.

The wee lady who lives in what appears to be a dungeon next door to our villa has just struggled up her stairway of tumbled rocks and passed me, waving an old straw hat and gasping, '*Molto caldo. Molto caldo.*'

So misleading. I keep scalding myself on taps marked '*caldo*'.

I can't believe I'm actually here after what were surely some of the worst weeks of my life.

It started when Mother washed the phone. She didn't manage to immerse it in the sink but she gave it a good going-over with a wet dish-mop. So it died. I didn't notice that it was just squatting there doing nothing till Dorothy-next-door struggled up the path to tell us we were 'unavailable'. I spent what seemed like two days in the phone-box at the corner with all the wrong change telling BT and getting the line tested. Dorothy-next-door struggled up the path again to tell us the line was perfectly all right so the fault must be in the house and a call-out charge was forty pounds. I opted for a horrible new hand-set from Gibsons in Dunoon.

The new disaster was Eleanor. She decided with great generosity of spirit to drive up and 'help with Aunt Mego'.

I thought it would be fun.

I thought it would cheer Ma greatly.

I thought wrong.

Mother turned. From a delightful dotty Mrs Jekyll she became a withdrawn and withering

Mrs Hyde. It was chilling. The night Eleanor cooked our supper for a treat, Mother pushed food around her plate with a disdainful fork and left the table. As I followed her to the sitting room she said bitterly, 'If I could find the frying-pan I would have cooked supper for myself.'

She wouldn't look at me.

'I know what you're doing, Phyllida. You're leaving me with Eleanor so you can go away.'

I put the television on.

Eleanor was exceedingly gracious and slipped gracefully into the background.

Then it was Claudia's turn.

Mrs Hyde struck again. At lunch one day, she patted Claudia's hand firmly and said, 'I don't know who you are – there must be some mistake, dear.'

It was always dangerous when Mother called anyone 'dear'. Leaving for her seat in the sitting room, she declared loudly, 'I can't live with her either.' I consulted everyone along the coast in a state of miserable panic.

I wondered then if her mood was drug-induced: it was so unlike her.

Mildew did some research into haloperidol and came up with a terrifying list of side effects, including 'heart failure, sudden death and pneumonia'. The more recognisable symptoms were 'sleep disturbances, restlessness and hallucinations'.

I remembered the time she wouldn't go to bed because there was 'a crowd of people on the stairs'.

Things sweetened a little with time. I came home from town one day to find Claudia, six feet in her socks, and little Mother making bread and wheezing over a recipe out of a wartime cookery book for an orange soufflé made with dried eggs and orangeade. 'As this is a highly nourishing dish in itself, it is especially suitable for serving after a rather scanty meal.' This made Mother shriek. 'Count one tablespoonful dried egg per person. Mix well each tablespoon of dried egg with one level teaspoonful of custard powder or plain flour. Per tablespoon of dried egg add a quarter of a pint of orangeade, which can be made with squash or essence. Stir well and bake – (or, worse) steam in boiling water till set.'

Then there was *chandeau* or 'Hot Foam' used in France as a festive pudding. How inconceivably frightful and very reminiscent of Ma's wartime sponge cake made with liquid paraffin.

But however good such moments were, Mrs Hyde was never far away. It was clear that Mother had smelt a Gigantic Rat.

It was me.

When she was safely in bed, the parlour turned into Bletchley Park, with maps, dates, plane bookings, ferry timetables, lists of phone numbers, diaries and *The Complete Works of Shakespeare*. I expect my guilt was written indelibly across my forehead. I was to play Ursula in *Much Ado*. It took me days to confess this treason. I chose a six o'clock cocktail time. 'Ma, I've been asked to be in the film of *Much Ado About Nothing*.'

'Oh, Phyllida! How thrilling. What's this we're drinking?'

I felt like poor blind Gloucester in *King Lear* throwing himself off the Cliffs of Dover and landing on his kitchen floor. I had finally 'come out'. Surprise and relief made me giddy. I sat by her side at supper, now and then guiding her fork in the right direction. Dainty and precise in her eating habits, her aim was less than perfect and she sometimes forgot just exactly where her mouth was. I told her my plans in different words. She had understood the first time, she told me. I never quite believed it, so I reminded her every day.

And here I am!

Aside from leaving vital equipment behind, I'd got on the correct plane, landed at Pisa, got on to an air-conditioned bus with other members of the cast and arrived at the location as required.

Final fitting yesterday evening when it was cooler. Very pleasing. The weight and swing of two heavily woven petticoats gives one poise. You can't sag. Lovely for dancing. (Rehearsal this evening.) All departments are housed under one beautiful roof. What bliss. Rumour has it that the property belonged to the family of the Mona Lisa, which means that Leonardo must have called in for tea with his paintbox and brushes. Mine have arrived via Make-up. I've packed them in a shoebox to smuggle on set.

There are two obese baby pigeons perched on the rafters outside Wardrobe, busy decorating a tailor's dummy with white poo and feathers. I'll paint them tonight.

———————

Got up this morning and walked into the kitchen barefoot, wearing the awful nightie that makes me look as if I've just escaped from an operating table, and there stood a tall dark stranger drinking coffee. We bowed. I left. It was Bertolucci. He'd come to see Keanu Reeves. When I told Sophie we were sharing with 'Keenoo Reeves', she almost needed medical attention. I'd never heard of him.

———————

Dance rehearsal. First go singing with Pat Doyle. Laughed till I wept.

———————

Up on the crown of a hill, all of us girls running down lickety-split in slippy leather sandals, dodging small boulders and twisted ankles and wheezing back up again for another go. Brian Blessed is charging up and down these rock-strewn precipitous hills, his pockets and rucksack filled with large stones, but he is training for Everest. He even meets wild boar. Apparently they are nimble and ferocious. Saw piles of their daintily shod legs at the butcher in Greve.

Another singing rehearsal tonight. Whoopee.

Picnic scene! No words. Bliss.

I sat very comfortably on a rug arrangement with sketchpad hidden under my skirts, a loaf of bread and an alarming-looking knife as props. It was my idea to cut slices against my chest as Gran used to do just as the camera slides by for a shot of Emma up a tree. Think now this is more Glasgow than Greve. Still, it was fun, and while complicated shots were composed, I remained staunchly in position, sketching the view.

Managed supper in a local restaurant last night. Spaghetti dish made with vodka. Horrid idea. Perfectly delicious.

nobody's at home...

Wonderful day off. One of those days that stretch time, only achievable when working on location and surplus to requirements. Neither Imelda nor I was called so we drove – well, she drove – over to see Richard Clifford in his villa up another hill. There we sat against a warm Tuscan wall, gazing at a view unaltered since da Vinci had chosen it for a background to one or other of his paintings. The odd conversational pearl changed hands and the kitchen wasn't far away.

Noël Coward said, 'You must be allowed to sleep as late as you like, slouch about in a dressing-gown for as long as you want, to meet as few strangers as possible and relax thoroughly in an atmosphere that is familiar, comfortable and without strain. This can only be achieved in the houses of loving theatre-minded friends – the hospitality of "civilians", however well intentioned, is too alien and strenuous for hard-working actors.' I always feel this rather harsh, and we didn't wear dressing-gowns.

In one of our shared silences, Imelda suddenly said, 'I remember my first tossed salad.' When we'd recovered from that, Richard remembered his ayah in India. I remembered my best friend. She and I played Daisy the Cow in *Aladdin*. She went on point in the front. I did tap at the back and was known as 'the udder half'. We were a sensation. She told me once that she knew she would die young. Furiously sceptical, I demanded (a) how she knew and (b) how it would happen. 'Will it be war, or will it be some accident like a chimney-pot falling on your head?'

'Something like *that*,' she said.

I've never been in Italy long enough to visit her grave and now everyone is dead who could tell me where it is. The newspaper headline someone sent me read 'Choreographer missing in Alps'. I didn't take it seriously for a moment. She'd turn up, laughing a lot. A week went by. There were heavy snowfalls in the region. They found her when it melted, curled up in a rocky crevice. The last photo in her camera was a bunch of gentians, 'Estelle Alpine'. She had bent down to get the close-up she had always wanted when a stone no bigger than a walnut fell from the melting ice on the high tops and split her skull. She was still warm from the snow cover so she was neatly folded into a rucksack and carried down like a baby by one of the guides to be buried in their tiny graveyard.

'*Ahora e una dei nostri*,' he said. I remember that. That, and don't ever climb the Alps at midday when the sun is out.

———

Rang home from the production office. Sophie answered. She's going to be there when I get back. Brilliant news.

———

Night filming. Masks, lanterns, wild music and a couple of fire-eaters. It looked wonderful. One shot was a mad rush altogether up a paved pathway towards the villa, passing the camera. My flip-flop leather sandals caught a bit of proud paving and I soared into the air and fell flat on my face. Filming stopped. A bag of ice was brought by an anxious nurse. My left eye closed quietly. We were all in the next shot, and I managed it rather unsteadily holding my mask at a critical angle over the worst.

At the wrap the first assistant director scanned my wounds, anxiously assessing whether my face could ever be seen on camera again. Mistaking the look for sympathy, I told him firmly I was perfectly all right. Someone brought me a mirror. I looked like a portrait by Lucien Freud. Green, purple, and crimson lake. I had split one nostril and my top lip; the whole of my left cheek and forehead were neatly skinned and livid. My left eye and anything to do with it had disappeared.

Dicky Briers and I were to leave on the earliest flight next day so there was no point in going to bed. I packed with one eye on a peerless dawn and sat in the early sun to await my pick-up, hoping the gentle warmth was healing. It was not. Dicky rooted around in his hand luggage and produced a crushed, accordion-pleated tube of Germolene on which he gave an unusually grave eulogy. I slathered it all over my wounds and balanced my sunglasses tenderly on my battered nose.

holding my mask at a
critical angle

The stewardess must have been appalled, but she never said a word, assuming, I suppose, that I'd had rather an intense domestic or half a face-lift. Sophie, wide-eyed, put me to bed in the Bothy where I slept for twenty-four hours.

———••———

Mego is in hospital. I am 'not to worry'. Her right eye went what the doctor called 'nasty'. There was talk of another trabeculectomy, or 'trabby', as it's commonly called. Ma thought it was the doctor's cat. More immediately, the girls had doubts about her chesty cough; Soph decided not to tell me. She thought it sounded a bit dramatic and, in any case, I hadn't been told about her own mumps when I was working in South America. True. I suppose it was sensible.

I'm told Ma said she had always wanted a 'real break' in the 'cottage hospital' so that the doctor could see what happened to her. When she came out, she announced, she would go to her 'old house ... not the one Phyllida put me in'. She was even thinking of 'taking a caravan'. When I sat beside her in the ward she introduced me to Sophie as 'Phyllida Law, the actress who likes walking about'. I held her hand. 'Am I supposed to eat this?' she asked.

Sitting next to each other, Soph said, Ma and I looked like some strange Norse god with two heads and one eye each. She has provided Ma with a visitors' book, which is already well used. All the Golden Girls have called in and so has the minister. A nurse has written that Ma enjoyed porridge for breakfast and asked for a whisky to follow. Nurse said it was eight a.m. 'That's never stopped me before,' Ma said. Apparently she got very cross when they gave her a bath. She called them 'a bunch of rotters', adding, 'Anyone would think I was a pair of socks.'

Dr W reminded her apparently that she had been asking him for a *coup de grâce* for fifteen years. A long run.

'Well, it's not *fair*,' she said.

My God, it's not, is it?

No whisper of hope or comfort reached us. It was a little like what it must have been with HIV

and AIDs – something you might avoid discussing with an elderly aunt, although a couple of mine would have loved it. I remember I threw away my wedding present of aluminium saucepans, which were supposed to last a lifetime, because there was a rumour that they could give you this foreign complaint no-one knew how to spell, which affected your brain and your personality. Mildew's Uncle Bill got it, swore a lot and became rather violent. Keep your saucepans. That scare was a myth. There's a lot of those about. I managed to understand the word 'dementia'. Mother didn't. She thought dementia was a friend of mine, but she would repeat in mild and accepting tones that she had 'somebody else's brain'.

Mildew asked good questions and sent me Quiz List No. 2, which was somewhat more advanced than the original set.

I'd already practised counting backwards. This one was very male. 'How heavy is a standard hammer?' I weighed ours. It was one pound eight ounces. 'How heavy is a full grown elephant?' I don't know but I'd love to see one on a weighing machine. The elephant I worry about is not only full-grown, it's in the front room with Mother. Is her condition hereditary? Some days it seems very likely.

Quiz No.2 continued:

'How many camels are there in Holland?'

'How fast does a commercial jet fly?'

'How long is an untied necktie?' Perhaps a female version would ask you about cup size.

Mr Naidoo had to do a test to become a British citizen and none of us knew the answers to any of the questions.

'How much is a first-class stamp?'

'What are the Queen's titles?' There were lots.

I've failed at citizenship but I am pursuing research into the terrible twins Dementia and Alzheimer's. I know there are experts, as Mother would call them – communicating, sharing, discovering and illuminating – but all that information never seems to percolate in our direction. It's like Mrs Thatcher's theory of wealth: she said it would accumulate at the top and trickle downwards. It doesn't, does it?

Difficult to know where and how to look for the answers but, feeling as out of place as a cabbage in a petunia patch, I went to a talk given by a professor to a room full of experts who understood 'lateral thinking' and 'cognitive estimation'. The Prof was very positive. 'It's good news,' he said. 'Alzheimer's is not an inevitable irreversible condition. It's a disease like, say, TB. Not only can it be treated, it can be cured.' It will be overcome. Not next week. Perhaps not in my lifetime but perhaps in my daughters'.

Rather cheered by Ma's request to Sophie to buy face-powder, puff, perfume, and half a dozen golf clubs.

As I left this evening she called, 'Don't forget the key to life.'

'What is it, Ma?'

'It's inside you.'

That's Buddhist, isn't it?

'Salvation lies in the fathom length of your own body.'

———

Rang production office to verify dates. I've got the scene with Brian Blessed first, I know, but I wondered if they really needed me for the final dance sequence. I'd get home two to three days earlier, if not. Could I perhaps skip it? They said I couldn't. It was only a faint hope.

———

Sophie has gone. It is very lowering. She is best at coaxing Ma to chat and reminisce. Her memories appear like those vivid bunches of flowers magicians produce from nowhere. We even got a revised list of her boyfriends. Gully Wishart, Tennant Cranston, Nesbit Evans and Norrie Dunlop. We are planning to get her a DVD of *Four Weddings and a Funeral* so she can see Soph. 'I don't know,' she said to a nurse, 'how I am supposed to get to four weddings and a funeral on the same day.'

———

Never travel without a tube of Germolene. Soph said before she left that she had witnessed a miracle cure. Eye back. Skin back. Remarkable. Tiny scar on nose and a bump on my lip but nothing that make-up can't hide. So that's a relief. I did, however, have a bit of a nervous breakdown. Hatched a plan to get Ma home before I left again but no one approved. She is in for drug reassessment and a new antibiotic for her chest – she may

the same. No Mego. 'Yoo-hoo' and 'Hello' were there, and Maisie with her knitted dolly on her knee glared at me and said, 'You and your crowd. Have you got the potatoes yet?' The woman who asked me for fifty pounds to 'get her out of here' seemed asleep in her chair.

Bessie was knitting. 'She's been calling and calling,' she said, raising her eyes to Heaven.

Out in the corridor a nurse called from a loo doorway. 'She's been moved to the ward by Sister's desk, Phyllida.'

That was where Uncle Arthur died.

There she was. Sound asleep. I dumped my bag, my shopping and the box of Cadbury's chocolate Swiss rolls, or whatever they were, and sat down to read the visitors' book. Eight days of notes and quotes.

Ma: 'I went to the theatre a lot when I was young, liked it better than the cinema.' That's a new one. I wouldn't have thought Grannie allowed such frippery.

'I can't spit, I'm too old.'

'Fruity cough persists': Mary M.

'My eyes don't tell me where I am.'

'Eyes tight shut but talking all the time': Claudia.

'Radiant toothless smile this morning': Beggsie.

'Come on! You're to start! Pick your spoons up.'

'Don't pay any attention to the rules. Ridiculous.'

'Very comfy and all scented on her sheepskin. Fed with a syringe like a wee hedgehog': M.

'Still worried about her frying-pan': P.

'Fast asleep but a bit restless': M.

'4.20 p.m. Slight temperature': P.

I woke when the visitors' book slid to the floor, with my chin on my chest and dribbling. Bent to pick up the book and laid my head on Ma's bed.

Breathing quick and shallow.

Chest bubbly.

Sister came in. She took Ma's hand. 'Phyllida's here.'

A tiny smile. 'That's nice.' A tiny voice.

'She got a wee temperature this afternoon.'

'Does it hurt, Ma?' I asked.

She made a little humming noise.

'She'll sleep,' Sister said. 'See you tomorrow morning.'

'I'll go home and get some too,' I said.

What is it about grief, even unacknowledged grief, that causes this utterly overwhelming exhaustion? A form of sleeping sickness. A coward's narcolepsy. It's a powerful avoidance technique. A flat denial.

I drove home to the cottage slowly and carefully, afraid of accidents. I left everything in the car, felt my way to Ma's bed, pulled off my shoes and trousers, lay down under the quilt and lost consciousness till about five a.m.

I was woken by a firm thump on my chest. I lay there listening to the seagulls jeering at me. Another thump. Wind? I hadn't eaten much yesterday.

I wandered into the kitchen and put the kettle on. No milk, of course.

The phone rang. It was Sister. 'I think you'd better come, Phyllida.'

I couldn't find the car keys. So I was late. Maybe by ten minutes. Maybe less.

The bed looked empty except for her little nose. 'As sharp as a pen.'

Sister had written in the visitors' book. 'Goodbye, Mego. I will miss you': Pam.

In John Mortimer's play *A Voyage Round My Father*, someone asks the son how he felt when his father died. He says one word: 'Lonely.'

That's quite good, isn't it?